T0332700

STRUCTURE LEVEL ADAPTATION FOR ARTIFICIAL NEURAL NETWORKS

THE KLUWER INTERNATIONAL SERIES
IN ENGINEERING AND COMPUTER SCIENCE

KNOWLEDGE REPRESENTATION, LEARNING AND EXPERT SYSTEMS

Consulting Editor

Tom Mitchell
Carnegie Mellon University

STRUCTURE LEVEL ADAPTATION FOR ARTIFICIAL NEURAL NETWORKS

by

Tsu-Chang Lee
Stanford University/
Cadence Design Systems

foreword by

Joseph W. Goodman
Stanford University

Kluwer Academic Publishers
Boston/Dordrecht/London

Distributors for North America:
Kluwer Academic Publishers
101 Philip Drive
Assinippi Park
Norwell, Massachusetts 02061 USA

Distributors for all other countries:
Kluwer Academic Publishers Group
Distribution Centre
Post Office Box 322
3300 AH Dordrecht, THE NETHERLANDS

Library of Congress Cataloging-in-Publication Data

Lee, Tsu-Chang, 1961-
    Structure level adaptation for artificial neural networks / by Tsu
-Chang Lee; foreword by Joseph W. Goodman.
        p. cm. -- (The Kluwer international series in engineering and
computer science. Knowledge representation, learning, and expert
systems)
  Includes bibliographical references and index.
  ISBN 0-7923-9151-9
  1. Neural networks (Computer science) I. Title. II. Series.
QA78.87.L443   1991
006.3--dc20   91-2251
                                              CIP

Printed on acid-free paper.

Printed in the United States of America

This book is dedicated to

my parents

    Ying-Jian Lee

    Chou-Feng Lu

my wife

    Yih-ching Salina An

and my daughters

    Teresa Tai-yi Lee

    Jennifer Jen-yi Lee

Contents

List of Figures

List of Tables

Foreword

My own introduction to the field of neural networks came with my discovery of the papers by J. Hopfield in the early 1980's (I am a newcomer to the field). Hopfield's combination of a linear matrix-vector multiplier and nonlinear feedback had an attractive simplicity, and seemed to capture the essence of a kind of system I had not encountered before. Associative memories based on basin of attraction raised interesting questions of convergence and storage capacity. The proposed optical realizations of such structures were particularly fascinating to me.

My level of sophistication improved when I learned about multilayer networks and the back-propagation training algorithm. The adaptive nature of neural networks became a property of paramount importance. Applications to various kinds of pattern recognition problems, including handwritten signature verification, occupied my attention. Nonlinear decision surfaces became possible. The power and flexibility of the neural network model had increased significantly.

Reading this book by T.-C. Lee has raised my level of understanding a great deal further. The concept of *Structural Level Adaptation*, through which the actual structure of the neural network adapts to the problem being solved, is a considerable step beyond the mere adaptation of weights. Under this paradigm, the detailed structure of a neural network is formed during training, and adapts to the particular training set presented. The structure of the network is no larger or smaller than required by the problem at hand, at least to the extend that this problem is properly represented by the training sequence. Neurons are generated or annihilated, depending on whether they are actually needed for the problem of interest. If, during the course of time, the statistics of the input change, the structure of the network can adapt in response.

The applications of the Structural Level Adaptation approach are still in the exploratory phase. A particular application discussed here by T.-C. Lee, with interesting results, is an adaptive vector quantization source coding system. Possible future applications to speech and/or image coding are certainly worth investigation.

In summary, the Structural Level Adaptation approach presented in this book raised my understanding of neural networks to a new level. I recommend the book to anyone who is seriously interested in broading his perspectives on this expanding field.

Joseph W. Goodman
Stanford, California

Preface

Current artificial neural network (ANN) models allow the networks to adjust their behavior by changing the interconnection weights associating neurons to each other, but the number of neurons and the structural relationship between neurons must be set up by system designers and once the structure is designed, it is fixed throughout the life cycle of the system. This sets quite a constraint on the applicability of artificial neural networks.

This monograph proposes a general framework for *Structural Level Adaptation (SLA)* of ANN to allow a neural network to change its structure in addition to weights in the adaptation process. Basic requirements and criteria for SLA of a ANN are identified and analyzed and a general paradigm, called *Activity Based Structure Level Adaptation (ASLA)*, is developed for SLA of ANN (chapter 2). Two structural level adaptable neural network models, FUNNET (FUNction NETwork) (chapter 3) and SPAN (Space PArtition Network) (chapter 4), are introduced to demonstrate the proposed SLA framework.

Software simulators for SPAN and FUNNET based on doubly linked lists were implemented and tested. Simulation results for the two different network models show that we can initially put a small number of seed neurons in the network, then let the neurons replicate and organize the structural relationships between one another according to the training patterns; finally the network grows to a configuration suitable to the class of problems characterized by the training patterns. In other words, the neural network self-synthesizes to fit the problem space. If the statistics of the problem space changes with time, the network will adapt its structure to follow the variations.

An adaptive source coding system based on SPAN is developed and computer simulation demonstrates that fast encoding/decoding, good rate-distortion performance, and smooth & incremental adaptation can be achieved using SPAN model (chapter 5). Potential applications of this coding scheme are speech and image coding as well as data compression for HDTV and ISDN systems.

The main contribution of this work is that we have provided a general framework for structure level adaptation of artificial neural networks, and we have demonstrated the validity of the proposed framework through two structural level adaptable neural network models (SPAN and FUN-NET), and the application of SPAN to some practical problems.

The material presented in this book basically follows my Ph.D dissertation at Stanford University. There is a long list of people who gave me supports and helps during my study at Stanford. First of all, I would like to extend my sincere appreciation to my thesis advisor, Professor Allen M. Peterson, for his encouragement and support throughout this study. Special thanks go to my reading committee, Professors Joseph W. Goodman, Peter M. Banks (now in university of Michigan), and Allen M. Peterson for reviewing my dissertation, as well as serving on my oral examination committee. Thanks also go to Professor John F. Vesecky for serving on my oral examination committee.

I wish to thank the past and present members of our research group, including Yen-jen Oyang, Kyon Choi, Viral Tolat (Vip), Adetokunbo

Ogunfunmi, Jim Burr, and others, for their friendship and stimulating conversations. My sincere appreciation goes to our excellent staff, especially Sieglinde Barsch, for doing all the real work.

I appreciate Professors James D. Meindl (now in RPI) and James D. Plummer for their support during my early years of study at Stanford. I would like to thank my friends Jane Yun-jen Hsu, Jemm-yue Liang, Hsi-Sheng Chen, Jye-Cherng. Tsai, Lawrence Rauchwerger, Steve Jurichichi, and Protheep Balasingam for their friendship which accompanied me throughout my study at Stanford.

To my family, this book is dedicated. My parents, Ying-Jian Lee and Chou-Feng Lu, have given of themselves without reservation that I could have the opportunity to attend Stanford. My wife, Yih-ching Salina An, has given me her constant love and support, without which, none of this would have been possible. I am also deeply in debt to my twin daughters, Teresa and Jennifer, for the first six months of their life which they have allowed me spend with the computer rather than with them.

This research was supported in part by NASA CASIS program under contract number NAGW-419 and in part by an unrestrict fund from Ford Aerospace and Communication Co. Mr. Lou Chall of Ford Aerospace is gratefully acknowledged for making the cooperation with Ford Aerospace possible.

Stanford, California   T.-C. Lee

STRUCTURE LEVEL ADAPTATION FOR ARTIFICIAL NEURAL NETWORKS

Chapter 1

Introduction

1.1 Background

The neural network, as a field of scientific research, can be traced back to the 1940's [13]. After the pioneer researchers established the basic models of the neural network experimentally [74, 51, 52, 57] and theoretically [89, 103, 50, 116, 121, 134, 95], this field remained an active field of research for about 26 years (1943-1969) . These first 26 years can be considered the *first period* of neural network research.

1969 is a very important separation point for the neural network field. In this year, Minsky and Papert published the book *Perceptrons* [95] which analyzed in detail a single-layer artificial neural network model (Perceptron, proposed by Rosenblatt [116]) and pointed out the limitation of this simple computation model. After this publication, the funding agencies like DARPA cut off the research fund, because they thought that the capability of neural networks was restricted by the profile sketched in *Perceptrons*. As a consequence, most research activities moved toward the *symbol-based* approach [45] and research in this ini-

1

tially active field diminished with only a small number of researchers remaining in this field of research [64, 49, 11, 38]. But in the meantime, computer vision became an active area of research; both the symbol-based approach and neural network paradigm were used [87, 88, 85]. This situation lasted for about 16 years (1969-1985) and will be referred to as the *second period* of neural networks.

Recently, this field has become the center of focus again. This is partly due to the development of multi-layer learning algorithms [108, 9], which enable the network to learn using a more complex structure to handle the kind of problems shown to be unsolvable in *Perceptrons* [95]. Another important reason for the revival of neural network research is that more internal dynamics of the network is revealed through insights into the fundamental laws governing the convergence of the group behavior of interacting physical elements [53, 54]. Now in the third period of its life cycle (1985-), neural network research has grown rapidly and has become one of the hottest topics within almost all the societies of IEEE. Special issues have been published [127, 34, 7, 6] and large conferences with thousands of attendees have been held [1, 2, 3, 5, 4]. Participating in this trend, DARPA initiated a neural network study to re-evaluate the potential of neural networks as the candidate model for our next generation signal processing or artificial intelligence applications [29]. This study also surveyed in detail the availability of the current technology basis for neural network development. This time the conclusion was more favorable to the neural network approach than it would have been 20 years ago.

However, there are still some major limitations on the capability of current neural network models. The most important of them is the *structure constraint*. Because an artificial neural network can only change the interconnection weights, and its structure has to remain fixed, the network designer faces the difficult task of figuring out the optimum structure of the network, thus placing a very tight limitation on its adaptability. I call the problem stated above the *Frame Problem* of artificial neural networks.

The main purpose of this book is to introduce the concept of **Structure Level Adaptation (SLA)** for artificial neural networks, and to establish the theoretical framework for this new paradigm. Applications and implementations of the SLA paradigm are also addressed in this study.

1.2 Neural Network Paradigms

Artificial neural networks serve two purposes:

- To study neuroscience based on a synthetic approach: The progress in neurobiology & neurophysiology has revealed many basic mechanisms to us. However, to understand how the brain works, in particular, how different sensory signals are processed and how cognitive processes work in the brain, requires further study on the system level. This is not an easy task to perform experimentally owing to the complexity of the system. To tackle the complexity problem, artificial neural networks serve as vehicles to carry on system level investigations. The idea is to synthesize low level findings and system level hypotheses together into an integrated system model, to test the model through computer simulation (or hardware implementation, like Mead's *silicon model* for neural networks [92]), and then to compare the performance with the behaviors of living systems [120].

- To build artifacts that display "brainlike" behavior: From an engineering point of view, the following features of the brain behavior supplement the weakness of performance of current artificial systems.

    - **Associative retrieval of information (B.I)**: Compared to artificial information processing systems, nerve systems display much greater capability to match and retrieve patterns associatively. Many simple pattern matching tasks (e.g., recognizing faces or identifying speakers), trivial to human beings, turn out to be extremely difficult, if not intractable, to machines.

    - **A small number of processing cycles to reach results (B.II)**: The neuron process is intrinsically slow, normally on the order of milliseconds [70, 56]. However most of the basic mental processes (e.g. perceptual processing, memory retrieval, language processing, and intuitive reasoning) can be done within several hundred milliseconds [110]. This suggests that these tasks must be done within 100 neuron process steps [35, 106]. Notice that most of our current signal processing applications require orders of magnitude more computation steps to complete the job.

    - **Graceful degradation with damage & information overflow (B.III)**: From the study of brain lesions and other forms of brain damage, we learn that the performance of the brain gradually deteriorates as more and more neural units are destroyed with the damage; therefore, there is no single critical point where the performance breaks down [74, 119]. Also, as more and more information is stacked into the brain such that the capacity of the brain reaches overflow (in the short-term sense), the patterns stored in the brain become vague; however none of the information is totally lost [107]. This graceful degradation behavior is attractive because as our engineering artifacts become more and more complicated, assuring complete correctness of their components becomes harder. Actually, this problem was foreseen long ago by von Neumann [100]. He remarked that there are two ways of building artifacts. In the first way, the correctness of the system behavior relies on the correctness of all the components in the system. If the error possibility of each component is p and there are N components in the system, then the error probability of the system is $e = 1 - (1 - p)^N$. As N grows larger, e grows closer to 1 and the only way to decrease e is to decrease p. This would require our fabrication technologies to generate higher yield and more reliable components. However, there is an unbreakable lower bound for p, which is set up by the fundamental laws of statistical mechanics and quantum mechanics. As our technology improves, the complexity of the system increases, and thus the requirement for p will move closer to the fundamental limit. In the second way of building artifacts, each component contributes something to the correctness of the system performance; in order for the system to be totally incorrect, all the components in the system need to be incorrect. For this kind of system, the possibility that the system is totally incorrect is $e = p^N$. The brain belongs to the second kind, but most of the current engineering artifacts belong to the first kind. As we approach the physical limit of technology, the design paradigm must shift to the second kind.

- **Learning behavior (B.IV)**: One of the most important
  characteristics of human intelligence is that we can improve
  our performance through learning. A more amazing fact is
  that the brains can be gauged through training to display similar performances even given many differences in the underlying hardware structures. This *gauged learning* is the basis
  of language, communication and education. On the contrary,
  for most of the engineering artifacts, the hardware structure is
  really crucial to the system behavior. For example, in VLSI
  manufacturing, we need to have very tight process control
  in order to achieve acceptable system performance. This is
  because small process fluctuations may propagate to become
  large circuit performance differences. This problem becomes
  more and more difficult as the device feature size becomes
  smaller and smaller.

As engineers, we are more interested in the second purpose listed
above, i.e. we want to grasp the essence of low level signal processing
mechanisms and organization of the brain to try to incorporate these
mechanisms into the design of our next generation artifacts. Following this approach, a group of design styles totally different from traditional ones are generated. These new approaches are basically a set of
paradigms distilled from nature's self-organization processes, in particular *mental processes.*

The following are the most commonly seen neural network paradigms:

- **Massively parallelism (P.I)**: The brain achieves its fast convergence behavior through massive parallelism by using a large

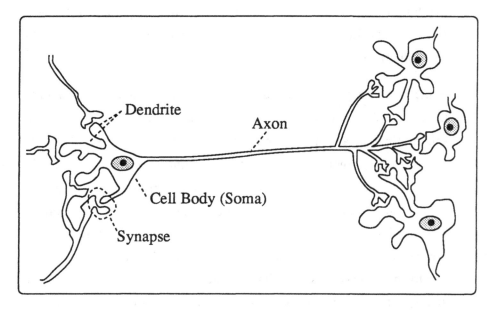

Figure 1.1: Schematic diagram of a neuron. The neuron receives input signals through synaptic contacts on its dendrite tree and generates action potentials which travel down the axon.

number of processing elements, and the system behavior is the result of the cooperative activity of many relatively simple processing elements. Each processing element is called a neuron. Current estimates hold that there are on the order of 10^{10} to 10^{11} neurons in the brain. It is well known that parallelism is necessary for high throughput computation systems. The speed of light sets the upper bound for the processing speed of sequential machines to be 1 BIPS for a 1 foot long machine, but many applications require 100 to 1000 BIPS [71].

- **Simple basic processing unit (P.II)**: The basic processing unit in a neural network is called a neuron. Figure 1.1 shows the schematic diagram of a neuron, which is a *summing-thresholding* element that aggregates a group of input signals (in the form of ionic current) from its dendrite tree; the input currents are integrated by the membrane capacitor of the cell body (soma) to depolarize the voltage across the membrane [1] until a critical *threshold potential* is reached, at which point an output signal is generated in the form of nerve pulses, called the *action potential.* These output strings of pulses propagate down the axon, which ends in a tree of synaptic contacts to the dendrites of other neurons [16, 70, 84]. Because of this switch-like behavior, most of the earlier neural network models suggest that the neurons work like a binary switch [89, 134, 116, 18, 95].

- **Knowledge representation in interconnection weights (P.III)**: The information in a neural network is stored in the form of *synaptic efficacy* at the synapse contacts between neurons [124, 125]. The

---

[1]In the non-active state, the membrane of the soma is charged and inputs from the dendrites will cause discharging of the membrane capacitor.

efficacy of a synaptic contact has the effect of controlling how much of the pre-synaptic signal (the action potential) can be transformed to the post-synaptic signal (the ionic current) to be integrated by the membrane capacitor of the cell body. This process is normally modeled as a multiplication between the pre-synaptic signal and the synaptic weight. There are two kinds of synaptic contacts: *excitatory* and *inhibitory*. For an excitatory synapse, the pre-synaptic signal helps to generate action potential, while for an inhibitory synapse, the pre-synaptic signal will cause the ionic current to flow in such a direction as to inhibit the generation of action potential. Excitatory and inhibitory synaptic contacts are modeled by positive and negative synaptic weights respectively.

- **Imprecise low level signal representations (P.IV):** The low level mechanism of the brain is imprecise in three ways:

  - Signal representation: The signal representation in the brain is imprecise. It is suggested that one byte (256 levels) suffices for representing the long-term strength of each synapse [118].

  - Wiring: The level of wiring in the nerve system has low accuracy and does not show any highly artificial interconnection patterns.

  - Processing: The signal processing on the neuron level is imprecise and noisy. This is because human tissue (or the "wetware") is a much more random medium than carefully fabricated silicon chips.

Because the function of the brain does not rely on precise, noise-free components and organizations, naturally, the nerve system can display highly fault-tolerant behavior.

- **Mixing of distributed and specialized representation (P.V)**:
  It has been argued sinced the 1940's whether the pattern representation in the brain is distributed (like holograms) or specialized (in which someone's *grandmother cell* may fire whenever his
  grandmother is in the scene). Studies in neural biology and neural
  physiology reveal that both distributed and specialized representation coexist in the brain. Generally speaking, each specific pattern
  is represented distributedly by a group of neurons, but different
  groups of neurons that are sensitive to different patterns do exist.

- **Highly distributed control (P.VI)**: There seems to be no global
  control mechanism in the brain to synchronize and coordinate the
  function of different components in the system. The behavior of
  the system is not the product of a prespecified computation algorithm, but rather is the emergent result of the local interaction
  between components. The major computation mode of the nerve
  system is *relaxation* rather than algorithmic procedures. Actually,
  distributed computation may become a trend for future complex
  systems. For example, in designing VLSI circuits, as the packing
  density increases, it is more and more difficult to enforce global
  timing and control signals over the whole system. People start
  thinking about asynchronous design style [91, 93]; this approach is
  attracting more and more attention in VLSI logic design as well.

- **Hebbian association rules (P.VII)**: 100 years ago, Williams
  James found that learning is a process of associating different concepts. He remarked:

  > When two brain processes are active together or in im-
  > mediate succession, one of them, on reoccurring tends to

propagate its excitement into the other [60].

Hebb later put this idea in the neural network framework:

> When an axon of cell A is near enough to excite a cell
> B and repeatedly or persistently takes part in firing it,
> some growth process or metabolic change takes place in
> one or both cells such that A's efficiency, as one of the
> cells firing B, is increased [50].

The essential concept suggested by this learning paradigm is used by almost all the current artificial neural systems. However, there are several different variations which we can categorize into three types:

- **Type 1 (P.VII.I)**: The amount of change in the synaptic weight is proportional to the product of the presynaptic signal and the output of neuron, i.e. $\Delta w_{ij} \propto x_j y_i$, where w_{ij} is the jth synaptic weight of neuron i, x_j is the presynaptic signal on the jth synapse of neuron i, and y_i is the output of neuron i. This is the simplest version of Hebbian learning. Example artificial neural network models utilizing this kind of learning are Brain State in a Box (BSB) [14, 15] and the Boltzmann Machine [9].

- **Type 2 (P.VII.II)**: The amount of change in a synaptic weight is proportional to the product of the pre-synaptic signal and the difference between the desired output and the real output of neuron i, i.e. $\Delta w_{ij} \propto x_j e_i$ where $e_i = (t_i - y_i)$ is the output error in which t_i is the desired output for neuron i. Notice this kind of learning requires the desired outputs (or the output error); hence it is a *supervised learning*. The famous network examples of this kind are Widrow's MAD-LINE [134, 135, 138] and Rumelhart's feed-forward error back-propagation network [108, 109].

– **Type 3 (P.VII.III)**: The amount of change in synaptic weight is proportional to the product of the output of the neuron and the difference between the pre-synaptic signal and the weight of the neuron, i.e. $\Delta w_{ij} \propto (x_j - w_{ij})y_i$. In this kind of learning, the synaptic weight vector of a neuron tries to follow the pre-synaptic vector (the input vector to the neuron) to which this neuron is sensitive; after enough training time, the weight vector of a neuron converges to the centroid of the input vectors *recognized* by this neuron. This type of learning is used in Grossberg's ART (Adaptive Resonant Theory) [49, 19], in Cohen & Grossberg's Masking Fields [24], and in Kohonen's SOFM (Self-Organization Feature Map) [65, 66].

• **Topological mapping (P.VIII)**: A phenomenon common to most of the sensory regions on the cerebral cortex is that neurons are arranged in some geometric order on a one or two dimensional sheet [12, 57, 130, 96, 111, 85]. The spatial order of neurons on the sheet usually reflects the order of the sensory patterns to which they are sensitive. A famous example is the direction sensitive *column structure* observed on the visual cortex of vertebrates. Here the neurons in the visual cortex are arranged in columns [57]. All the neurons within a column are sensitive to line segments in the same direction and adjacent columns are sensitive to similar segment directions [58, 59]. Many researchers have proposed artificial neural network models and learning algorithms to explain how this ordered mapping is formed [85, 86, 136, 137, 65].

Figure 1.2 shows the relationship between brain behavior features and neural network structural and operational paradigms. A link between a behavior feature item and a paradigm means that the paradigm contributes to that behavior feature item.

1.3 The Frame Problem in Artificial Neural Networks

The ability to learn is the most important property of an artificial neural network. In most of the current artificial neural network models, learning is done through modification of the synaptic weights (using the Hebbian learning rule) of neurons in the network. This kind of learning is basically a *parameters adaptation process*. The network designer must specify the framework in which the parameters resides. Specifically, the designer has to decide the number of parameters and the relationships between parameters in the system. Once the framework is decided, the system works like a iterative spread sheet, with each parameter represented by a table entry and the relationship between parameters specified by equations relating table entries [133].

However, choosing a suitable frame for the parameters to reside in is sometimes a difficult task, especially in an unknown environment. Even if we can choose a frame in the beginning of system relaxation, later on if the problem's characteristics change, the system might not be able to process the problem further. The following lists some observations which contribute to the frame problem:

- **The network structure design problem is non-trivial**: Neural networks in nature are not designed but evolved. From genera-

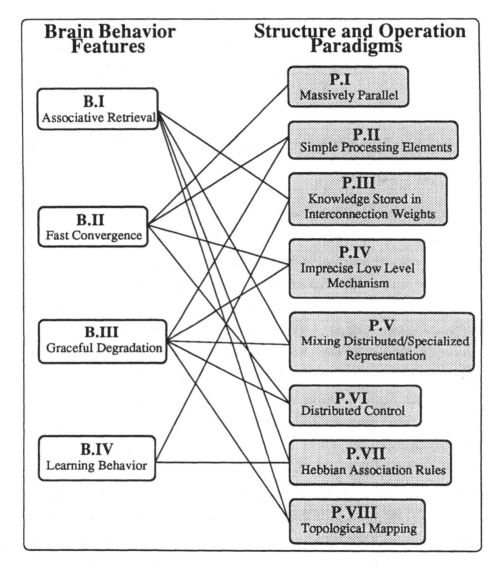

Figure 1.2: The relationship between neural network paradigms and brain behavior features.

tion to generation, the system learns its structure through interaction with its environment. This structure learning process not only happens in the long-term evolution process but also in the development process of an individual body [31, 32]. If we consider gene codes as the *blue-print* for the final form of a living creature, this blue-print only specifies partial information for the final structure, because the chromosomes do not have enough space to specify all the structural details of a brain. Because the structure of a nerve system is evolved and developed rather than pre-specified, it would be very hard to grasp the function-structure relationship of the brain [2] and try to map it into the design of engineering artifacts. This suggests that if we really want to build adaptive artifacts that can display more sophisticated brain-like behavior (e.g., cognition, language and symbol manipulation ability), we have to follow a design path that allows the system to develop its structure through interaction with its environment.

- **System adaptability is limited by the network structure**: For a fixed structure network, the network capability is restricted. If the problem changes in size, the network might not be able to *scale up* to meet the requirement set by the new problem because the processing capability of a network is limited by the number of neurons in the system. Even if the problem doesn't change in scale, it might change in *contextual characteristics* and would require a different organization of neurons to do the job. To handle this, we have two choices:

---

[2] Most of our current understanding about the brain are in the low sensory level; the relationships between most of the high level functions and the brain structure are still unknown.

1. To make the size of the network large enough to accommodate all possible variation in the problem scale, and to design the structure of the network with enough sophistication to process all possible changes in the problem context.

2. To allow the network to adapt its structure according to the short-term (relative to the whole life cycle of the system) characteristic of the problem.

If we choose the first solution, we will meet the network design problem again, because for more complicated problems with unpredicatable characteristics, designing such a universal structure is a very difficult, if not impossible task.

- **Artificial computing resources are limited**: Compared to neural network systems in nature, our current artificial computing resources are very limited [3]. Because of this, we must be very careful in utilizing computing resources when planning artificial neural network structures. Hence it would be more desirable for a network to adapt its structure to utilize resources only as required by short-term problem characteristics, rather than to allocate all the resources that would ever be required in its whole lifetime to the network all the time.

---

[3]There are about 10^{11} neurons and about 10^4 synaptic inputs (in average) for each neuron in the brain. If each synaptic weight has the accuracy of 1 byte, the memory requirement to implement a brain is of the order of 10^{15} bytes. This is equivalent to 10^9 memory chips using state of the art VLSI manufacturing technology.

1.4 Approach

Because of the *frame problems* listed in the previous section, we want to allow the system to adapt its frame in addition to parameters. This leads to the idea of *adaptable structure* neural networks, which is the main purpose of this thesis.

Two things need to be made adaptive in order to have an adaptable structure network:

1. The number of neurons in the network, and

2. The structural relationship between neurons in the network.

To adapt the two items listed above, the following paradigms are helpful:

- **Paradigms from information theory**: Information theory has been applied to estimate the capacity of complex data processing structures like decision trees [22]. Recently, some people have also applied this paradigm to estimate the capacity of neural networks [23, 90]. Basically, a neural network can be considered a framework on which to form the representation for some stimulus-response relationships for the problem of interests. The tradeoffs between representation complexity and representation accuracy can be considered from the *distortion-rate* point of view. Hence the ideas and results from information theory, such as rate-distortion theory [17, 39, 122, 123, 132] and minimum description length principle [112, 113, 114, 115] are helpful for building artificial neural network models with adaptable representation frames.

- **Paradigms from biological systems**: Studying the evolution and development processes of biological systems can reveal how the

structures are formed through interaction with the environment of
the living systems in nature. These structural adaptation mechanisms in biological systems can suggest ways of building adaptable
structure artifacts. In particular, the following facts are observed
from the early development process of the brain [55, 120, 31, 32]:

- Neurons are mobile in the beginning of the brain development
  process. In the initial phase of the brain formation process,
  a neuron is mobile and can migrate from its original position
  to the proper position in the cortex. This migration process
  is guided by the interaction with local tissues along the migration path.

- After the earliest phases of embryonic development, a neuron
  throws out *projections* (its dendrites and axons to-be) to form
  interconnections. Experiments reveal that if the synaptic connections made by a group of neurons are destroyed by cutting
  the axons connecting these synapses to their originating cell
  bodies, the axons of nearby neurons will sprout to form new
  connections with those neurons originally connected to the
  destroyed neurons. The above experiment suggests that the
  interconnection formation is a *competitive growth* process that
  involves close interaction between neurons.

- A massive cell death occurs immediately after birth. In newborn mammals, about 15 percent of the neurons present in
  the neonate die in early infancy. Most of these neurons die
  because improper connections are formed between them and
  other neurons in the network and therefore they are unable to
  receive the electrical or chemical stimuli needed to keep them
  vital.

Besides development, the process of evolution can also suggest the basic mechanisms through which the forms of different organisms emerge [33, 8, 141].

- **Paradigms from physics**: Outside the biological world, we also observe many self-organizing structure development processes [8, 141]. The following are examples from the physical world: the crystal growth and particle diffusion process studied in solid state physics [62] and the phase transition process studied in statistical mechanics [63, 104]. In fact, many researchers are already applying paradigms from physics to engineering artifact design. For example, *spin glass* models have been used [94, 61] to model neural network systems and to solve combinatorial optimization problems; also various people [53, 54, 36] have applied the energy concept to model the convergence behavior of neural network systems.

When structure level adaptation capability is added to an artificial neural network system, the system performance is characterized by the relaxation behavior on 3 levels:

1. **Function Level Adaptation:** Changing the output activity levels of neurons in the system according to the input signals and the interaction between neurons.

2. **Parameter Level Adaptation:** Adapting the synaptic weights in the network within the framework set by structure level specifications.

3. **Structure Level Adaptation:** Adapting the network structure according to the statistics of the variables in the parameter and function levels.

Throughout this book, I will take the multi-level adaptation point of view stated above to formulate, analyze, and propose solution to the problems. All the formalisms and models proposed in this thesis are for neural networks with *discrete time dynamics*.

1.5 Overview of This Book

The tree structure shown in Figure 1.3 outlines the conceptual relationships among the important entities proposed in this monograph. Every node in the *contribution tree* represents a knowledge entity which is new to the field of neural networks up to December, 1990. The knowledge entities outlined in Figure 1.3 are distributed in 4 chapters as stated below.

Chapter 2 lays down the formal conceptual structure for *Multi-Level Adaptation* of artificial neural networks. Within this formal structure, a structure level adaptation paradigm called *Activity-Based Structured Level Adaptation (ASLA)* is introduced as a general guideline for structure level adaptation of artificial neural networks. Chapter 2 also describes a method for analyzing the structure of neural networks to find out the minimum delay to ensure the consistency of states in the network. Basically, this chapter forms the *Ontology*[4] of discrete time neural networks from the multi-level adaptation point of view.

Chapter 3 applies the basic framework defined in Chapter 2 to multilayer feed-forward neural networks. An adaptable structure multi-layer neural network, *FUNNET (FUNction NETwork)*, is defined. A mea-

---

[4]The term "Ontology" originally means "the essence of being" in metaphysics. People in AI research adopt this term to mean the essential objects and their relations in a particular field of knowledge (ontology study is the pre-step of building any expert system for knowledge engineers). Here I use this term in a similar sense.

sure, called *Fluctuated Distortion Measure (FDM)* is introduced to guide the structure level adaptation process for FUNNET. A dynamically adjustable data structure based on doubly linked lists is proposed as the basic representation framework for FUNNET. A software simulation tool is implemented based on the proposed data structure.

Chapter 4 defines a class of competitive signal clustering neural networks with adaptable structures—*SPAN (Space PArtition Network)*. The parameter level adaptation processes are analyzed and a theorem, called the *SPAN convergence theory*, is described. The structure level adaptation procedures are also proposed and analyzed. A flexible data structure that can support all the structure level operations for SPAN is introduced. This representation scheme forms the basis of a software simulator for SPAN.

Chapter 5 introduces an adaptive vector quantization source coding system based on SPAN. A variable rate coding scheme, called the *Path Coding Method* is proposed to reduce the redundancy in the source signals in order to enhance the rate-distortion performance. A fast codebook searching method is introduced to decrease the encoding/decoding time. The process for dynamically adjusting the structure of the codebook on both the transmitter and the receiver sides is also described.

Relevant theorems and measures are listed in the appendixes. Proofs are supplied for the new theorems proposed in this book; however only the facts are stated for the theorems with existing proofs.

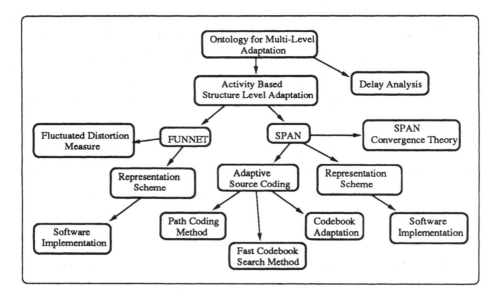

Figure 1.3: The contribution tree of this book.

Chapter 2

Basic Framework

2.1 Introduction

The main purpose of this chapter is to identify the conceptual entities needed to specify a *discrete time* neural network and to put them together in a formal mathematical structure, i.e. to construct the *Ontology* for neural networks. This ontology study allows us to achieve the following goals:

- to built a general conceptual structure for neural networks that can cover most of the current models.

- to supply a basic framework for designing, analyzing and implementing neural network architectures.

- to propose a method to calculate the minimum delay required for a neural net to propagate the effects of input signals to the output port.

- to formalize the multi-level adaptation process for neural network systems. In particular, I defined the concept of "Structure Level

Neural Networks", which are networks capable of changing their structures autonomously.

In defining this concept, I adopt two basic viewpoints:

1. Information Representation Point of View: I define the items in my conceptual structure based on an information representation point of view. To be more specific, I define the variables in my model based on the consideration of what data entities are necessary to specify the general idea of a neural network.

2. Multi-Level Model: According to the variables allowed to change, we can classify neural networks into three levels: **Structure Level (S-Level)**, **Parameter Level (P-Level)**, and **Function Level (F-Level)**, with plasticity decreasing in order. An S-Level neural network becomes a P-Level network with some variables specified, and a P-Level network becomes an F-Level network with some additional parameters specified.

The body of this chapter is divided into four parts. Through part one (Section 2.2) and part two (Section 2.3), I define the general ideas of neurons and neural networks up to the P-Level. The conceptual structure outlined in these two sections covers most of the current neural network models. In part three (Section 2.4), I go further to define the S-Level neural networks and the related concepts, such as *neural network space*, *bases for neural network space*, and to outline the concept of *multi-level adaptation* for artificial neural networks. In part four (Section 2.5) I introduce the **Activity-Based Structure Level Adaptation (ASLA)** paradigm, which can be used to guide the structure level adaptation process of artificial neural networks. Finally, based on the activit⁼   ᶜ various processes in the P-Level and the F-Level, I introduce the basic S-Level mechanisms, that will be used throughout this book.

2.2 Formal Neurons

A discrete time **Formal Neuron (FN)**, is specified by the 5-tuple

$$N =< F, Q, W, \Gamma, C >;$$

this is defined by the following:

F, called the **State Tansition Function (STF)**, is a **Parameterized Function Tree (PFT)** [1] with modulating parameter structure W. F is used to generate the **Composite State (CS)**, Q, of this neuron with $Q = F(\vec{x} \mid W)$, where the vector $\vec{x} = (x_1, x_2, \ldots, x_m) \in \mathcal{F}_1^m$ designates the list of input arguments for F ($\mathcal{F}_1$ is the field [2] corresponding to the input variables of this neuron). The set of input arguments $X = \{x_1, x_2, \ldots, x_m\}$ is called the **Receptive Field (RF)** of this neuron. The function tree F is specified as follows [3]

$$F = (f \underbrace{(f_1 \ \cdots)}_{C_1} \underbrace{(f_2 \ \cdots)}_{C_2} \cdots$$
$$\cdots \underbrace{(f_k \ \cdots (f_{k.\tilde{p}} \ (f_{k.\tilde{p}.1} \ \cdots) \ (f_{k.\tilde{p}.2} \cdots) \cdots) \cdots)}_{sub-tree \ C_k} \cdots$$
$$\cdots \underbrace{(f_n \ \cdots)}_{C_n}),$$

where every $f_{\tilde{h}}$ (called the **Node Function (NF)**) in F is a member of $\mathcal{H}$

---

[1] or the equivalent tree of a **treelizable** graph, to be defined later.

[2] e.g. the set of integers, $\mathcal{Z}$, or the set of real numbers, $\mathcal{R}$.

[3] I use $(r \ C_1 \ C_2 \ \ldots)$ to represent a tree with root r and $C_1, C_2, \ldots$ are sub-trees under r. I use $(\phi \ T_1 \ T_2 \ \ldots)$ to represent a forest of trees $T_1, T_2, \ldots$. A single node tree is of the form $A = (e)$, where e is the only element in A.

(called the **Function Space (FS)** for this neuron), which is the set of all possible functions for $f_{\tilde{h}}$'s ($\tilde{h}$ denotes the path from the root to $f_{\tilde{h}}$ in F). There is an input argument vector $\vec{a}_{\tilde{h}} = (a_{\tilde{h}1}, a_{\tilde{h}2}, \ldots, a_{\tilde{h}m_{\tilde{h}}})$ associated with each function $f_{\tilde{h}}$ in F. The set of arguments $M_{\tilde{h}} = \{a_{\tilde{h}1}, a_{\tilde{h}2}, \ldots, \}$ is called the **Input Argument Set (IAS)** for $f_{\tilde{h}}$. The input arguments for the leaf functions $f_{\tilde{a}1}, f_{\tilde{a}2}, \ldots$ are selected from the RF of F ($M_{\tilde{a}} \subseteq X$) if $f_{\tilde{a}}$ is a leaf in F. Every leaf function $f_{\tilde{a}}$ is a mapping from $\mathcal{F}_1^{||M_{\tilde{a}}||}$ to $\mathcal{F}_2$. [4] The root function f of F, denoted by $Rt(F)$, is a mapping from $\mathcal{F}_2^{||M_0||}$ to $\mathcal{F}_3$, where M_0 denotes the input argument set for the root function of F. Besides root and leaves, each of the other nodes $f_{\tilde{b}}$ is a mapping from $\mathcal{F}_2^{||M_{\tilde{b}}||}$ to $\mathcal{F}_2$. The symbols $\mathcal{F}_2, \mathcal{F}_3$ represent the fields corresponding to the internal and output states of this neuron respectively.

The composite state Q is a tree structure, specified as follows

$$Q = (q \underbrace{(q_1 \ \ldots)}_{S_1} \underbrace{(q_2 \ \ldots)}_{S_2} \cdots$$
$$\cdots \underbrace{(q_k \ \ldots (q_{k.\tilde{p}} \ (q_{k.\tilde{p}.1} \ \ldots) \ (q_{k.\tilde{p}.2} \ldots) \ldots) \ldots)}_{sub-tree \ S_k} \cdots$$
$$\cdots \underbrace{(q_n \ \ldots))}_{S_n},$$

where every $q_{\tilde{h}}$ in Q represents the output of a node function $f_{\tilde{h}}$, i.e. $q_{\tilde{h}} = f_{\tilde{h}}(\vec{a}_{\tilde{h}})$. There is a one to one correspondence between the elements in F and the elements in Q.

W is a forest, called the **Modulating Parameter Structure (MPS)** for F, specified by

---

[4] I use $||S||$ to denote the number of elements in set S.

$$W = (\phi \underbrace{(w_1 \ldots)}_{T_1} \ldots \underbrace{(w_2 \ldots)}_{T_2} \ldots$$

$$\ldots \underbrace{(w_k \ldots (w_{k.\tilde{p}} (w_{k.\tilde{p}.1} \ldots) (w_{k.\tilde{p}.2} \ldots) \ldots) \ldots)}_{tree\ T_k} \ldots$$

$$\ldots \underbrace{(w_n \ldots)}_{T_n}).$$

Each parameter $w_{\tilde{p}.i}$ in W is used to modulate the output of function $f_{\tilde{p}.i}$ (i.e. $q_{\tilde{p}.i}$) through a **Modulating Function (MF)** $g_{\tilde{p}.i}()$. The modulated output $g_{\tilde{p}.i}(q_{\tilde{p}.i}, w_{\tilde{p}.i})$ of $f_{\tilde{p}.i}$ is fed to the father node $f_{\tilde{p}}$ as an input argument. The input argument list of a non-leaf node function is the list of all the modulated outputs of its child functions, i.e., [5] [6] [7]

$$a_{\tilde{p}i}[*] = g_{\tilde{p}.i}(q_{\tilde{p}.i}, w_{\tilde{p}.i})[*], \ 1 \le i \le Arg(f_{\tilde{p}}), i \in \mathcal{Z}^+.$$

Each parameter $w_{\tilde{p}}$ in W is defined over $\mathcal{F}_2$.

At any time index n, the inputs to neuron N, designated by $In(N)[n]$, are the values presented in the RF of this neuron; the output of N, designated by $Out(N)[n]$, is equal to the state value $q[n]$, which is the output from the root function f of the function tree F, i.e. $In(N)[n] = \vec{x}[n]$, $Out(N)[n] = q[n]$. Notice that $In(N)$ is defined over $\mathcal{F}_1^{Dim(In(N))}$ and $Out(N)$ is defined over $\mathcal{F}_3$. [8] The signal flow path from the input port through F to the output port is called the **Feed Forward Path (FFP)** of neuron N.

---

[5] For a time varying element η (a scalar, vector, structure, function, etc.), I use $\eta[n]$ to denote it's value at time index n. I adopt the convention of using $*$ to denote the current time index, so $\eta[*]$ means the current value of η and $\eta[* - 1]$ means the value of η at the previous time index.

[6] $Arg(f_{\tilde{p}})$ denotes the number of arguments for function $f_{\tilde{p}}$.

[7] $\mathcal{Z}^+$ is the set of positive integers.

[8] I use $Dim(\vec{X})$ to represent the dimension of vector $\vec{X}$.

Γ, called the **Parameter Adaptation Automata (PAA)** of neuron N, is specified by a pair $< \delta, \sigma >$.

δ, called the **Parameter Adjusting Function (PAF)** (or in conventional terminology, **learning function**) of neuron N, is a mapping that takes $In(N)[*]$, $W[*]$, $Q[*]$, $C[*]$, and $e_{in}[*]$ as inputs to generate $W[*+1]$. i.e.,

$$W[*+1] = \delta(\vec{x}[*], Q[*], W[*], e_{in}[*], C[*]),$$

where $e_{in} \in \mathcal{F}_1$, called the **Received FeedBack Signal (RFBS)**, is the feedback signal received from the output port of neuron N.

σ, called the **Parameter State Transition Funciton (PSTF)** of neuron N, is characterized by the following:

$$C[*+1] = \sigma(\vec{x}[*], Q[*], W[*], e_{in}[*], C[*]),$$

where C, called **Parameter Control State (PCS)** of neuron N, is a structure of variables used to control the parameter adjusting process (or learning process) of this neuron. $\vec{e}_{out} \in \mathcal{F}_1^{Dim(In(N))}$, called the **Transmitting FeedBack Vector (TFBV)**, is the list of feedback signals, called the **Transmitting FeedBack Signals (TFBS)**, to be transmitted upstream to the RF of neuron N. There is a one to one correspondence between the variables in RF and the components of $\vec{e}_{out}$. The path of signal flow from the output port through δ to the input port is called the **FeedBack Path (FBP)** for neuron N.

The definition of formal neurons stated above gives a very general picture of a neuron to be used as a computation element and covers most of the current neural network models. The basic ideas are depicted by Figure 2.1 and Figure 2.2. Figure 2.1 shows the block diagram of the formal neuron defined above. Notice the two levels of signal flow (F-Level and P-Level) indicated in this diagram. Figure 2.2 shows the general form of the function tree in this neuron.

The general computation requirement for STF F is a **treelizable**

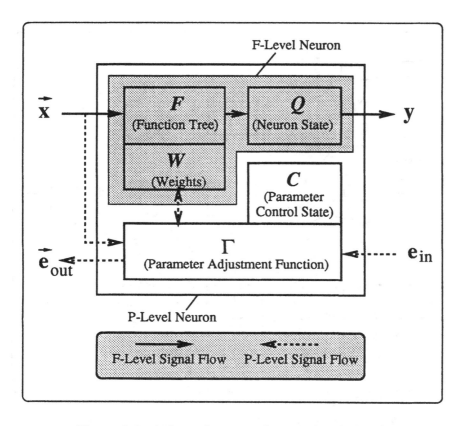

Figure 2.1: A formal neuron (up to the P-Level).

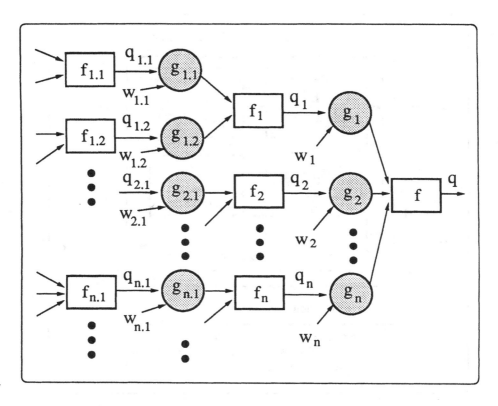

Figure 2.2: The function tree of a formal neuron.

graph structure of functions. **"Treelization"** means to convert the function graph to a tree without changing the input/output relationship of the function graph. Figure 2.3 shows an example of converting a function graph to its equivalent tree. The following corollary tells when a graph is treelizable.

Corollary 2.1 :
A **non-cyclic function graph** *(i.e. a graph of functions without cycles) is treelizable.*   ◇

The biological counterpart for F is the dendrite tree observed in biological neurons [84, 56]. The main purpose of F is to collect information from the RF and to make associations between variables in the RF through the tree structure of functions.

A special function D_k, called the **time index shift function**, can be included in F. The following equation defines D_k: [9]

$$a[* - k] = D_k(a[*])$$

where k, called the *shift index*, is an integer. A time index shift function $D_k()$ with k greater than zero is called a **delay function**. We can traverse the function tree F (Figure 2.4), starting from the root variable, to assign relative time index to the node variables according to Algorithm 2.1.

Algorithm 2.1 (Temporal Dependency of Input-Output Signals) :

1. *Assign $q[0]$ to the output of the root.*

---

[9]Mathematically, this might not be considered a function, but an operator. Here I use the term "function" in a very general sense to mean any mapping that maps a set of input objects to a set of output objects.

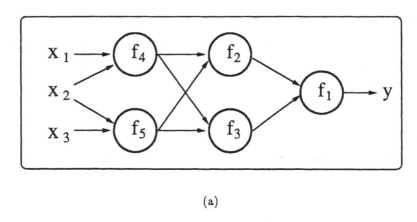

(a)

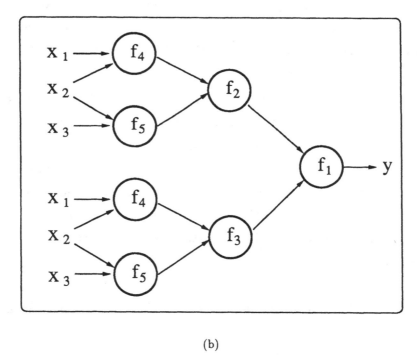

(b)

Figure 2.3: Treelize a function graph. (a) The original function graph (b) The corresponding tree.

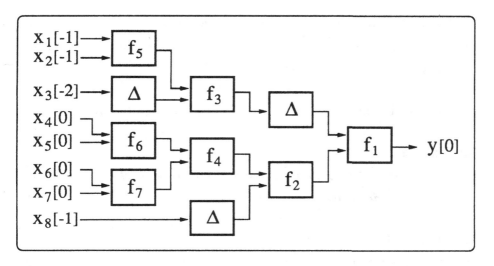

Figure 2.4: Decide the temporal dependency of the variables in a function tree.

2. *Traverse the tree in preorder* [10] *to visit every node in the tree exactly once. When visiting a NF $f_{\tilde{p}}$ with assigned output $q_{\tilde{p}}[d]$, we assign the index $d - i$ to the output variables of its child if $f_{\tilde{p}}$ is $D_i()$; otherwise we assign index d to the the output variable of its children NFs.* ◇

Figure 2.4 shows an example of relative time index assignment using the above algorithm. After traversing the F tree using the above algorithm, we can obtain the time indexes of input variables relative to the output variable of the STF for this neuron. The following definition describes the input-output temporal behavior of a neuron:

Definition 2.1 (Causality) :

Using the F tree traversal procedure defined by Algorithm 2.1, if all the

---

[10]i.e. first visit the root, then visit the sons [131].

input variables have indexes less or equal than zero, this neuron is called
causal*; if all the input variables have indexes less than zero, this neuron*
is called **strictly causal**.   ◇

Following Definition 2.1, we have the corollaries stated below.

Corollary 2.2 :
A neuron is causal if it does not contain any time shift function $D_k()$
with the shift index k *less than zero.*   ◇

Corollary 2.3 :
Neuron N is strictly causal if it does not contain any time shift function
$D_k()$ *with* $k < 0$ *and every path from its RF to the output contains at*
least one time index shift function $D_k()$ *with* $k \geq 1$.   ◇

The modulation function (MF) $g_{\tilde{p}}()$ is a delayless function, normally
in a very simple form. The most commonly seen form of $g_{\tilde{p}}()$ in most of
the current neural network models is "product", i.e., $g_{\tilde{p}}(q_{\tilde{p}}, w_{\tilde{p}}) = q_{\tilde{p}} w_{\tilde{p}}$.
Other examples of MF will be shown in Chapter 4.

For most cases, the node functions (NFs) in F are symmetric, i.e. if
two arguments of an NF, $f_{\tilde{p}}$, exchange positions with each other, $f_{\tilde{p}}$ will
still give the same result. Sometimes even the function tree F itself is
symmetric, i.e. if two variables in the receptive field exchange position
with each other, the neuron will give the same output. When the above
condition is satisfied, the neuron is called a **RF symmetric neuron.**
For example, a neuron with I/O relation $y = f(\sum_{i=1}^{n} w_i x_i)$ is an RF
symmetric neuron.

A neuron can have $\vec{e}_{out}$ and e_{in} eliminated from C; In this case,
it is called a **Uni-Directional Neuron (UDN)**. Formal neurons with
both $\vec{e}_{out}$ and e_{in} specified are called **Bi-Directional Neurons (BDN)**.

Normally BDNs are used in supervised learning networks. The neurons in the *error back-propagation* network [108, 109] are examples of this category.

Not all types of neuron learning process need to have PCS (Parameter Control State) specified. A learning mechanism with PCS specified is called a *learning mechanism with internal state*; a learning mechanism without PCS specified is called a *memoryless learning mechanism*.

The collection of all possible values of W for a neuron N,

$$< \ldots, W, \ldots >$$

forms a vector space, called the **Neuron Parameter Space (NPS)** for N. The property of this space is important for analyzing the parameter adaptation (or learning process, in conventional terminology) of a neuron.

2.3 Formal Neural Networks

A formal neural network is specified by the set:

$$G = \{A_1, A_2, \ldots, A_n\}$$

of **Network Elements (NE)**, with each network element a triple:

$$A_i = < N_i, R_i, T_i >,$$

the components of which are defined as follows:

N_i, called the **Processing Kernel (PK)** of A_i, can be either a formal neural network or a formal neuron.

R_i, called the **Input Connection Map (ICM)** for A_i, contains the fan-in interconnection information for A_i. During feed-forward operation, R_i assigns to each input argument x_{ij} of N_i one of the outputs from some PK N_k in G, or one of the input signals to the network, i.e.,

$$\forall x_{ij} \ in \ \vec{x}_i \quad = \quad In(N_i) \, (x_{ij} \overset{R_i}{\leftarrow} y_{km} : y_{km} \ in \ \vec{y}_k = Out(N_k)$$

$$for \ some \ PK \ N_k \ in \ G) \vee (x_{ij} \overset{R_i}{\leftarrow} u_k : u_k \ in \ \vec{u} = In(G)).$$

The set of NEs with some input arguments received from the inputs of the network is called the **Input Set (I-Set)** of the network. Each NE in the I-Set is called a **Neural Input Element (NIE)** of the network. The set of variables connected to N_i through R_i is called the **Receptive Field (RF)** of A_i.

T_i, called the **Output Connection Map (OCM)** for A_i, contains the fan-out interconnection information for A_i. During feedback operation [11], T_i assigns to each Received FeedBack Signal (RFBS) $\epsilon_{in,ij}$ of N_i one of the Transmitting FeedBack Signals (TFBSs) from some PK N_k in G, or one of the RFBSs of the network, i.e., [12]

$$\forall \epsilon_{in,ij} \; in \; \vec{\epsilon}_{in,i} \;\; = \;\; Rfb(N_i)(\epsilon_{in,ij} \overset{T_i}{\leftarrow} \epsilon_{out,km} : \epsilon_{out,km} \; in \; Tfb(N_k)$$
$$for \; some \; PK \; N_k \; in \; G)$$
$$\vee(\epsilon_{in,ij} \overset{T_i}{\leftarrow} e_{in,k} \in \vec{e}_{in} = Rfb(G)).$$

The set of NEs with outputs sent to the output port of the network is called the **Output Set (O-Set)** of the network. Each NE in the O-Set is called a **Network Output Element (NOE)** of the network. The set which contains all the variables connected to the output of a NE A_i is called the **Projective Field (PF)** of A_i.

For the feed forward path, the inputs to the network are the signals extracted from the external variables which are [13] connected to the input ports of the members in the I-Set of the network, and the outputs of the network are the signals generated by the members in the O-Set of the

---

[11] For bi-directional type of PK only. A network containing bi-directional PKs is called a **bi-directional network**.

[12] $Rfb(N)$ denotes the vector of received feed back signals (RFBSs) of processing kernel N. $Tfb(N)$ denotes the vector of transmitting feed back signals (TFBSs) of processing kernel N.

[13] External to the network.

network and connected to the variables external to the network. For the feed back path, the received feedback signals (RFBSs) of the network are the externally connected RFBSs of the members in the O-Set of the network, and the transmitting feedback signals (TFBSs) of the network are the externally connected TFBSs of the members in the I-Set of the network.

Figure 2.5 shows the general configuration of a formal neural network as defined above. From this definition of formal neural network stated above, a neural network can be hierarchically structured, i.e. it can be composed of smaller neural networks, each of which is composed of even smaller networks. As a matter of fact, a specific type of neural network can also be defined recursively just as I define the general concept of neural networks in this section.

Generally speaking, the data dependency relation in a neural network forms a graph structure. In such a structure, a phenomenon, called **state inconsistency**, may occur if the STFs of the neurons in the network are not arranged properly.

Definition 2.2 (State Inconsistency) :
For a general neural network system defined above, at any particular time index, given a set of input signals $\bar{u}$ and with the internal state S^- of the system before applying the input signals specified, if the state S^+ of the system after applying the input signals cannot be uniquely determined, then this network is said to be state inconsistent under state S^- and input $\bar{u}$. Networks of this type are called **state inconsistent networks.** $\diamond$

A hierarchically defined neural network can be flattened down to the neuron level by traversing down the multi-level interconnection specifications. A neural network is said to be **forestizable** if the network of

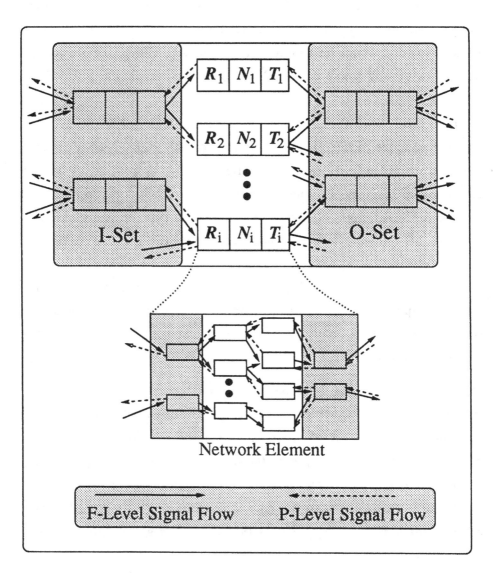

Figure 2.5: A formal neural network (up to the P-Level).

functions in the flattened version of the network can be converted to a forest with the input/output relationship of the network preserved. Each tree in the forest is rooted at a function that generates one of the outputs of the network. For a forestizable network, we have the following corollary:

Corollary 2.4 :
A forestizable neural network is state consistent if all the neurons in the network are causal. ◇

A state inconsistent neural network can be converted to a state consistent network by adding delay functions in the network. Figure 2.6 shows an example of such a conversion. The following corollary is useful for designing state consistent neural networks.

Corollary 2.5 :
A non-forestizable neural network is state consistent if all the neurons in the network are causal and there exists at least one strictly causal neuron in every cycle in the network. ◇

The corollaries above reveal a very important criterion for neural network structure design: when putting neurons together into a network structure, if the signal flow graph (i.e. the function interconnection graph) is forestizable, then the computation results of the network can appear on the output port at the same time index as the input signals; otherwise a delay function must be inserted into each cycle in the graph. In order to transform a state inconsistent network into a state consistent one, we need to identify all the cycles in the network. This is often a time consuming job. The following corollary gives a sufficient condition for the state consistency of a network.

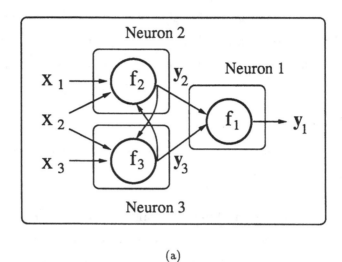

(a)

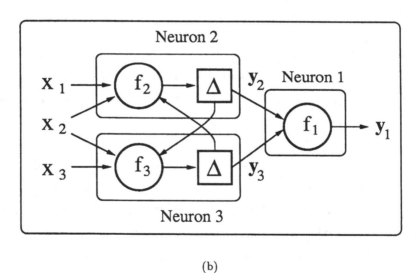

(b)

Figure 2.6: Eliminate state inconsistency by adding delay function. (a) The original state inconsistent network (b) The new network with delay functions added to retain state reconsistency.

Corollary 2.6 :

A neural network is state consistent if all the neurons in the network are strictly causal.   ◇

From Corollary 2.6, we know by simply adding delays to every non-strictly causal neuron to make it strictly causal, the state consistency of the network is assured.

By analyzing the functional graph of a neural network, we can calculate the minimum delay needed to propagate the influence of a set of input signals to the output port. This criterion, which I named the *consistent state criterion*, should be a guideline for neural network implementations, both software and hardware. For example, if we implement a neural network serially in software, for strictly causal neurons, we need to have two state variables q_i^- and q_i^+ associated with each neuron. In order to change the states of neurons in the network, we must visit each neuron two times, as shown in the two **for** loops in the pseudo-codes listed below:

Algorithm 2.2 (Strictly Causal Neuron State Transition) :

$\vdots$

loop {

    fetch next input signal for the network;

    for *(i = 1 to Number-of-Neurons)*

$$q_i^+ \leftarrow F_i(q_{R_1^i}^-, q_{R_2^i}^-, \ldots, q_{R_{Arg(F_i)}^i}^- \mid W_i) \; ;$$

    for *(i = 1 to Number-of-Neurons)*

$$q_i^- \leftarrow q_i^+$$

}

$\vdots$

$\diamond$

It is observed from neuro-biological study that there are map-like structures in different sensor regions on the cerebral cortex. The most famous one is the orientation sensitive column structure in the visual cortex [57, 58, 59, 85, 86]. It was shown that the cells within each column on the visual cortex are sensitive to line segments in a particular direction and adjacent columns are sensitive to slightly different directions. This direction of sensitivity changes continuously on the visual cortex as if the neurons are laid down on a topological map. The topological map allows artificial neural networks to sort out the adaptation parameters spatially in the learning process [66, 67, 68] by supplying a geometrical space in which to put the neural network. To be more specific, the neurons in a topological map "know" their positions in a geometrical space, at least relatively and locally. [14] This positional information of neurons is in general not specified in the formal neural network defined in the context

---

[14]This means a neuron knows its relative position to other neurons in the vicinity.

above. [15] This suggests the concept below.

Definition 2.3 (Topological Neural Network) :
A topological neural network is a pair $T =< G, M_H >$, where G is a formal neural network; M_H is a topological mapping that assigns to each neuron i in G a position vector $\vec{h_i} \in H$. H (called the **neuron topology space***) is a subset of some vector space V.*   ◇

A general continuous topological space for neural networks might not be easy to implement. It would be desirable to have a simple, regular space if we want to implement a topological neural network artificially. The following is a candidate:

Definition 2.4 (Lattice Neural Network) :
An n dimensional **Lattice Neural Network (LNN)***, $S =< G, M_U >$, is a topological network, in which the neuron topology space U for M_U is a subset of some lattice L, i.e.:*

$$U \subseteq L = \{\vec{r} = \sum_{i=1}^{n} b_i \vec{v_i} \mid (b_1, b_2, \ldots, b_n) \in \mathcal{Z}^n\}$$

where[16] $\vec{v_1}, \vec{v_2}, \ldots \vec{v_n}$ are a set of linear independent vectors, called the **Primitive Translation Vectors (PTV)** *of the lattice.*   ◇

2.4   Multi-Level Adaptation Formalism

The main purpose of the formal structure introduced in the context above is to put together the information needed to specify a neural network in an organized way, so that it may form the basis for software or hardware implementations of neural network models.

---

[15] The general neural net model specifies a neural net as a directed graph.

[16] $\mathcal{Z}$ is the set of integers.

In general, the variables in the formal neural network structure can change with time. The rules used to change the neural network variables are called *adaptation rules*. According to the different kinds of variables allowed to change, we can classify the network dynamics into 3 levels:

- **Function Level (F Level):** can also be called the *signal processing level*. In this level, only the state Q_i of neurons are allowed to change. Neural networks on this level are distinguished by the values of all the variables except Q_i's, i.e. two neural networks are considered the same if they have different values for Q_i's but the same values for all the other variables. Neural networks on this level are called **F-Level neural networks (F-Net)**. The network dynamics on this level are characterized by the state transition of the variables Q_i of the network. The Hopfield net [53, 54] is an example of this level.

- **Parameter Level (P Level):** can also be called the *parametric learning level*. In this level, not only Q_i's, but also the neuron parameter structure W_i's are allowed to change. Networks with Q_is and W_is different, but everything else the same are considered to be the same on this level. Neural networks on this level are called **P-Level neural networks (P-Net)** The network dynamics on this level are characterized by the traces of parameters in neuron parameter spaces (NPS). The majority of current neural network models which are able to learn are on this level. The important examples are, Kohonen's Self-Organization Feature Map [66, 67], Widrow and Hoff's Madline [134], Grossberg's ART [49], Ackley and Hinton's Boltzmann Machine [9].

- **Structure Level (S Level):** can also be called the *structural* *evolution level.* On this level, besides F-Level and P-Level variables, the neural networks are allowed to change other variables that specify the structure of the network. In particular, the network is allowed to change the interconnections between neurons, generate neurons or annihilate existing neurons in the network. Currently, very few models allow a neural network to adapt itself on this level.

Basically, the S-Level adaptation transforms a P-Level neural network to another P-Level neural network. Any transformation that does this is called a *Structure Level Operator*. To put the ideas into a more rigorous conceptual structure, I offer the following definitions:

Definition 2.5 (Neural Network Space) :
A neural network space $\mathcal{N}$ is a collection of formal neural networks (up to the P-Level, as defined in Section 2.3). An operator over a neural network space is a mapping that transforms a neural network $S_i \in \mathcal{N}$ to a neural network $S_j \in \mathcal{N}$. ◇

Definition 2.6 (E-Space) :
*A **neural network structure evolution space (E-space)** is a pair $\mathcal{E} = < \mathcal{N}, \Delta >$, where $\mathcal{N}$ is a neural network space and Δ is the set of allowable Structure Level Operators (SOPs) for $\mathcal{N}$, where each SOP is a mapping that transforms a neural network to another neural network in the neural network space $\mathcal{N}$. $\mathcal{E}$ satisfies the following conditions:*

- *$\forall \mathcal{P}_i \in \Delta \ \forall N_j \in \mathcal{N}, \mathcal{P}_i(N_j) \in \mathcal{N}$. In other words, $\mathcal{N}$ is closed under Δ.*

- *$\forall \mathcal{P}_i \in \Delta \ \exists \mathcal{P}_i^{-1} \in \Delta \ (\forall N_j \in \mathcal{N} \ \mathcal{P}_i^{-1}(\mathcal{P}_i(N_j)) = \mathcal{P}_i(\mathcal{P}_i^{-1}(N_j)) = N_j)$. In other words, an operator $\mathcal{P}$ and its inverse $\mathcal{P}^{-1}$ must both exist in Δ.*

◇

Definition 2.7 (Reachability) :
In an E-space $\mathcal{E} =< \mathcal{N}, \Delta >$, two neural networks S_i and S_j are **reachable** *by each other (denoted by $\mathcal{R}(S_i, S_j)$) iff*
$$(\exists \mathcal{P}, \mathcal{P}^{-1} \in \Delta,\ (S_i = \mathcal{P}(S_j)) \wedge (S_j = \mathcal{P}^{-1}(S_i))).$$

◇

Definition 2.8 (Basis) :
A basis of an E-space $\mathcal{E} =< \mathcal{N}, \Delta >$ is a pair $\mathcal{B} =< \mathcal{S}, \Phi >$, where $\mathcal{S} \subseteq \mathcal{N}$ and $\Phi \subseteq \Delta$. $\mathcal{B}$ satisfies the condition: [17]

$$\forall S_i \in \mathcal{N}\ (\exists S_j \in \mathcal{S}\ \exists \mathcal{P} \in (\Phi)^+,\ S_i = \mathcal{P}(S_j)),$$

where $\mathcal{S}$ is called a **Base Set (BS)**, *and Φ is called a* **Spanning Operator Set (SOS)** *of $\mathcal{E}$.*   ◇

Definition 2.9 (Irreducible Basis) :
A basis $\mathcal{B} =< \mathcal{S}, \Phi >$ of an E-space $\mathcal{E}$ is **irreducible** *iff*

$$(\forall S_i, S_j \in \mathcal{S},\ \neg \mathcal{R}(S_i, S_j) \wedge \neg (\exists \mathcal{P} \in \Phi\ (\exists n \in Z^+\ \exists \mathcal{T}_1, \mathcal{T}_2,$$
$$\ldots, \mathcal{T}_n \in \Phi,\ (\mathcal{T}_1, \mathcal{T}_2, \ldots, \mathcal{T}_n \neq \mathcal{P}) \wedge (\mathcal{P} = \mathcal{T}_1 \mathcal{T}_2 \ldots \mathcal{T}_n)))).$$

When $\mathcal{B}$ is irreducible, $\mathcal{S}$ is called the **Minimum Base Set (MBS)**, *Φ is called the* **Primitive Operator Set (POS)**, *and each operator in Φ is called a* **Primitive Operator (PO)** *of $\mathcal{E}$.*   ◇

---

[17] For a set Φ, Φ^+ means the union of all the sets generated by the Cartesian product of Φ and itself, i.e.

$$\Phi^+ = \cup_{i=1}^{\infty} (\Phi)^i,$$

where $(\Phi)^i$ means $\underbrace{\Phi \times \Phi \ldots \Phi}_{i\ times}$, $\times$ is the Cartesian product operator for sets.

Corollary 2.7 :

$\mathcal{B} =< \mathcal{S}, \Phi >$ *is an irreducible basis for an E-space* $\mathcal{E} =< \mathcal{N}, \Delta >$. *If there are k elements in the MBS* $\mathcal{S} = \{N_1, N_2, \ldots, N_k\}$, *then* $\mathcal{E}$ *can be partitioned to k disjoint E-spaces* $(\mathcal{E}_1, \mathcal{E}_2, , \ldots, \mathcal{E}_k)$ *with bases*

$$\mathcal{B}_1 =< \{N_1\}, \Phi >, \mathcal{B}_2 =< \{N_2\}, \Phi >, \ldots, \mathcal{B}_k =< \{N_k\}, \Phi >.$$

$\diamond$

Definition 2.10 (Simple E-Space) :

An E-space $\mathcal{E} =< \mathcal{N}, \Delta >$ *is called a* **simple E-space** *iff* $\forall N_i, N_j \in \mathcal{N}, \mathcal{R}(N_i, N_j)$ $\quad \diamond$

Section 2.2 , 2.3 define the information structure needed to specify a P-level neural network. To specify an S-Level network (i.e. a neural network that can adapt itself structurally), we need to specify the mechanisms to modify network structures.

An S-Level neural network (**S-Net**) is specified by a 4-tuple $E =< G, \Phi, \Theta, J >$, the components of which are defined as follows:

G is a structure containing the specification of a P-Level neural network; Φ is a SOS (Spanning Operator Set) for the E-space $\mathcal{E}$ that G belongs to.

Θ (called the **Structure Evolution Automata (SEA)** for the S-Net, $\mathcal{E}$) is used for two tasks:

- To select a set of operators to act on $G[*]$, in order to generate the next P-Level network specification, $G[* + 1]$.

- To modify the internal state information needed for guiding the structure level adaptation process for the S-Net, E.

Θ is specified by a pair $< \eta, \xi >$.

η, called the **Structure State Trasition Function (SSTF)**, is a mapping which takes $G[*]$, $In(G)[*]$, $Rfb(G)[*]$, $J[*]$ and $\vec{c}_{in}[*]$ to generate $J[*+1]$. The vector $\vec{c}_{in}$, called the **Received Structure Control Vector (RSCV)**, contains the signals received from the environment [18] (other than the F-level and L-level signals) in order to control the S-level adaptation process of the network.

J, called the **Structure Control State (SCS)** of E, is a structure of variables used to control the S-level adaptation process. $\vec{c}_{out}$, called the **Transmitting Structure Control Vector (TSCV)**, contains the signals to be sent to the environment.

ξ, called the **Structure Operator Selection Function (SOSF)** for E, is a mapping that takes $J[*]$ as input to generate a list $D[*] = d1.d2.....d_k$ (called the **Structure Evolution Action List (SEAL)** for E) with each d_i in D a member of Φ .

Putting everything together, we have the following equation specifying the dynamics of an S-level network:

$$< G[*+1], J[*+1] >$$
$$= \Theta(G[*], In(G)[*], Rfb(G)[*], J[*], \vec{c}_{in})$$
$$=< \xi(J[*])(G[*]), \eta(G[*], In(G)[*], Rfb(G)[*], J[*], \vec{c}_{in}) >$$

The above definition of S-Level networks sketches the general structure of a neural network capable of adapting itself structurally (see Figure 2.7). Basically, an S-level network can be considered a higher level machine that takes the specification of a P-level machine (i.e. a neural network in the usual sense) as input in order to generate another P-level machine specification. The core of the whole process is the struc-

---

[18]The possible agents sending these signals are supervisors who monitor the evolution process of the network.

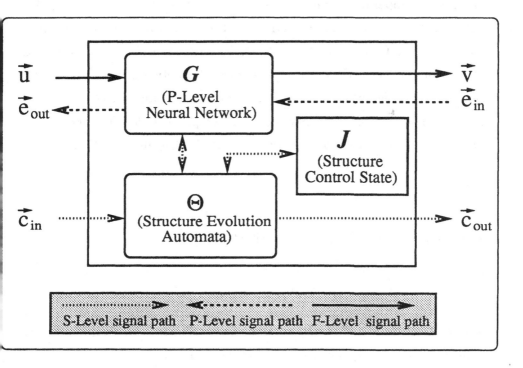

Figure 2.7: A structure level neural network with centralized control mechanism.

ture evolution automata Θ. Θ can be a centralized mechanism guiding the structure evolution process of the whole network, or can be distributed among the neurons throughout the network. In most of the self-organization systems in nature, the structure evolution mechanism seems to be quite distributed, i.e. the system behavior is determined by the group cooperative and competitive activities of the composing elements of the system [32]. In a **Distributed S-level Network (DSN)**, the Structure Control State (SCS) and Structure Evolution Automata (SEA) of the network are scattered over the network elements of the network. The definition of DSN is similar to the definition of the formal neural network defined in Section 2.3, except now the network $\mathcal{G}$ is a collection of **Network Structure Evolution Elements (NSEEs)**:

$$\mathcal{G} = \{B_1, B_2, \ldots, B_n\},$$

where each of the NSEE B_i is specified by

$$B_i = < A_i, \Phi_i, \Theta_i, J_i >,$$

where $A_i \in \Omega_i$ is a P-level neural network element; Ω_i is the network element space for A_i (i.e. the set of all possible A_i's). The definitions of Φ_i, Θ_i, and J_i are similar to those of S-Level neural networksl; basically, their purposes are to map the S-Net $\mathcal{G}[*] = \{B_1[*], B_2[*], \ldots, B_n[*]\}$ to $\mathcal{G}[* + 1] = \{B_1[* + 1], B_2[* + 1], \ldots, B_n[* + 1]\}$ through the interaction between the environmental variables and the variables in the NSEEs in $\mathcal{G}[*]$. Figure 2.8 shows the structure of an NSEE. In a fully distributed S-Level neural network, the Structural Operators (SOPs) are all defined on the neuron level, i.e. the basic NSEEs are neurons. In general, each NSEE can be a sub-network of $\mathcal{G}$.

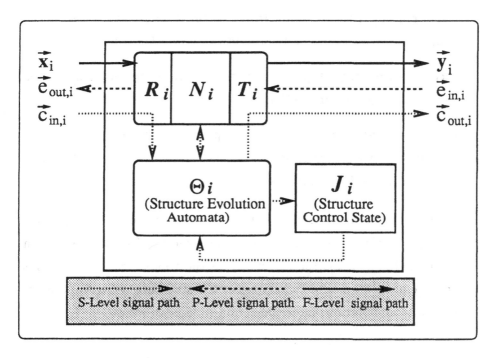

Figure 2.8: A network structure evolution element.

According to the general neural network architecture defined in this chapter, the neuron level structure level operators (SOPs) can be categorized into 4 classes:

- **Existence Operators**: generate neurons, kill neurons.

- **Function Tree Operators**: delete node functions from the tree; select a new node function from the function space $\mathcal{H}$ (the set of allowable node functions) and add the new NF to the tree.

- **Interconnection Operators**: modify the interconnection maps R_i and T_i defined in Section 2.3.

- **Topological Operators**: For topological neural networks, we should have an extra class of operators to modify the position of a neuron in the topological space.

With the set of operators Φ defined, we need to specify the operator selection process; i.e., we have to define the Structure Operator Selection Function (SOSF), η, for the S-Net. Here the topological relationships between neurons are useful to help select the structure related operators (generation/annihilation, interconnection modification, etc.).

2.5   Activity-Based Structural Adaptation

There are three important steps in defining a structure level neural network (S-Net):

Guideline 2.1 (S-Net Construction) :

1. *Define the E-Space for this S-Net: i.e., to identify the set of P-Nets that we want this S-Net to cover through structure level adaptation.*

2. *Specify the spanning operator set (SOS) for the E-Space: i.e., to define the set of network structure operators (SOPs) that can transform a network to another network in order to cover the whole E-Space.*

3. *Define the structure evolution automata (SEA) for the S-Net: i.e., to specify the automata that can select the SOPs from the SOS according to the structure control state (SCS) and other system status in order to guide the structure evolution process in the E-Space.*

An S-Net can be specified based on an existing class of P-Net. In most of the current artificial neural network models, a single neuron do not have much structure. To be more specific, each neuron in most models is just a multiplication-summing-thresholding element. For this kind of simple neuron, the intra-neuron structure can be considered fixed [19] and the following class of SOPs are sufficient to cover the network space:

- Neuron generation operator: generate a new neuron.

- Neuron annihilation operator: kill a neuron.

- Neuron structural relationship modification operators: change the structural relationship between neurons.

Once the structure level operators are defined, we need to determine the rules for applying those SOPs on a network structure. Neurobiological studies suggest that neural networks change their structure according

---

[19]Hence, we don't need to specify the complicated intra-neuron function tree operators.

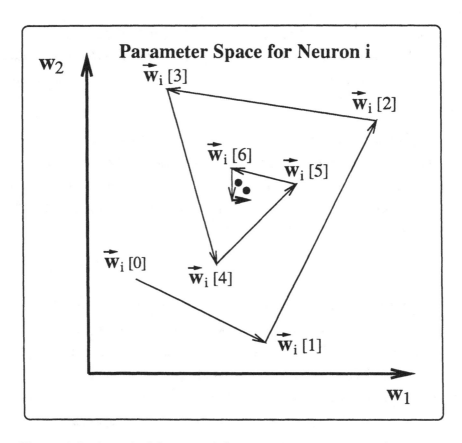

Figure 2.9: A typical input weight convergence process of a neuron.

to the *activity* of the objects in the network during the early phase of their life cycle. The migration of neurons, the growing of dendrite/axon trees during the embryonic development process, and the massive death of neuron cells during early infancy are all very closely related to the activity of different objects in the network. In this book, I propose to use this "object activity" as the paradigm for the Structure Level Adaptation (SLA). The mechanisms described in the following subsections are useful for SLA of neural networks in general.

2.5.1 Neuron generation

To help determine the criteria for the neuron generation process, I observe the following neural networks behaviors:

- If a neural network has enough neurons to process a class of problems, then during the training phase, the parameter structure [20] of each neuron will converge to a small neighborhood region around a certain value in the neuron parameter space (NPS).

- If the neural network does not contain enough neurons to learn a class of problems, then the parameters of neurons will tend to fluctuate greatly even after a long training period.

Figure 2.9 shows a typical input weight convergence process of a neuron in the neuron parameter space. Notice that during the convergence process, the average length of movement between adjacent temporal weight vectors in the parameter space is gradually decreasing. Based on this observation, I define a measure, called the **Walking Distance** (**WD**) for neurons:

$$WD_i[n] = \sum_{m=n-L+1}^{n} Met(\vec{\mathbf{w}}_i[m], \vec{\mathbf{w}}_i[m-1]) \qquad (2.1)$$

where $WD_i[n]$ is the WD for neuron i at time sequence n; $\vec{\mathbf{w}}_i[m]$ is the input weight vector to neuron i at time m; and Met is some metric

---

[20] In the most often seen simple neuron case, this parameter structure is just the input weight vector of each neuron. However in the most general case, this structure can become a tree, corresponding to the modulating parameter structure (MPS) of the function tree of each neuron.

that measures the distance between vectors in a metric space [21]. WD_i measures the short-term average length of the movement of the input weight vector of neuron i in the weight space within a temporal window of size L. In essence, WD_i is a measure for the time variation of the stored information for neuron i and can be considered the activity of neuron i in the parameter space. Too high a WD for a particular neuron indicates that the processing capability of the neuron is insufficient and that a new neuron is needed to share its load. Practical implementation of (2.1) requires the storage of L numbers for WD calculation. (2.2) shows a variation of (2.1) that can be more economically implemented:

$$WD_i[n] = \frac{\sum_{m=1}^n \gamma_w^{n-m} Met(\vec{w}_i[m], \vec{w}_i[m-1])}{\sum_{m=1}^n \gamma_w^m} \qquad (2.2)$$

Notice that (2.2) can be approximated by the following operational measure (see Appendix D for a derivation):

$$\widehat{WD}_i[n] = \gamma_w \widehat{WD}_i[n-1] + (1-\gamma_w)Met(\vec{w}_i[n], \vec{w}_i[n-1]) \qquad (2.3)$$

The above measure requires only one storage unit to store the current value of WD_i for each neuron. In equation (2.2) and (2.3), γ_w, a factor greater than zero and less than 1, is used to control the *effective temporal window* size in the averaging process. The closer γ_w is to one, the wider the effective temporal window size, and hence the more samples taken

---

[21] There are many different ways of defining metrics, the easiest one is the **Euclidean metric** defined as:

$$EuMet(\vec{X}, \vec{Y}) = \sum_{i=1}^N \sqrt{(x_i - y_i)^2}$$

where

$$N = Max(Dim(\vec{X}), Dim(\vec{Y}))$$

into the averaging process. Basically the WD defined in (2.2) represents a weighted average of the distance between temporally adjacent weight vectors. The weights $\{\gamma_w^m\}$ are set up such that more recent moving distances are emphasized in the averaging process.

Actually, equation (2.3) suggests the following general way for calculating the short term average for any random process $\{\xi[m]\}$:

$$\bar{\xi}[n]_\gamma \triangleq \frac{\sum_{m=0}^n \gamma^{n-m}\xi[m]}{\sum_{m=0}^n \gamma^m}$$
$$\approx \gamma\bar{\xi}[n-1]_\gamma + (1-\gamma)\xi[n] \tag{2.4}$$

Equation (2.4) is very useful in the structure level adaptation process, because as we will see in later chapters, many variables in the structure control state (SCS) to be used by the structure evolution automata (see Figure 2.7 , 2.8) are temporal averages of the various processes in the parameter level.

Since each neuron is a parameterized function, the fluctuation of its parameters will cause the fluctuation of its output values, and hence would contribute to the overall system errors. Based on this idea, we can define the neuron generation guideline as the following:

Guideline 2.2 (Neuron Generation) :
- *A neuron i should generate another neuron if*

$$\varepsilon_i \triangleq \frac{\partial\varepsilon}{\partial WD_i}\cdot WD_i > \Theta_G \tag{2.5}$$

where ε is the overall system error (or whatever cost function, depending on each specific neural network model), WD_i is the walking distance for neuron i, ε_i represents the contribution of neuron i to the overall system error owing to its parameter fluctuation, and Θ_G is some threshold value.

- *The newly generated neuron should inherit the same structure level attributes as its parent neuron.*

◇

2.5.2 Neuron Annihilation

Because the resources are limited in any phys cal computation environment, in order to achieve an overall good system performance, we must remove unnecessary components from the system. For the development process of biological nervous systems, Nobel Laureate Gerald Edelman suggests that the neurons in a network follow a process similar to evolution, in which Darwin's selection rule determines the survival of neurons in the early brain forming process [31]. Owing to the competitive mechanisms between neurons and the selection rule that keeps the neurons capable of finding their correct positions in the network and removes those misplaced ones, the network can gradually form a correct structure in the development process [22]. To be more specific, we have the following two observations:

- If a neuron does not form the correct interconnections between other neurons [23] then it will die in the early development process.

- Owing to the competition between neurons, the neurons fight with each other for resources; each neuron tries to inhibit other neurons from taking exactly the same functional role that it plays in the network.

---

[22] Of course, this is not to say that Darwinism is the only process in the development process; genetic information and the interaction with other body cells besides neurons also play important roles in the development process of nervous systems.

[23] Hence cannot be stimulated by appropriate input signals and is unable to keep sufficient output activity.

The above observations suggest the following guideline for the neuron annihilation process in artificial neural networks:

Guideline 2.3 (Neuron Annihilation) :
We can kill a neuron if:

1. *It is not a functioning element in the network.*

2. *It is a redundant element in the network.*

◇

For any neuron in a network, the first criterion above can be checked by monitoring the output activity of this neuron during the P-Level adaptation process. If the output activity is fixed over a very long P-Level adaptation process, then we know that it does not contribute to the function of the network, because it does not generate any information in its output. As the measure for the first criterion, we can use the variance of the output activity—VA (called *Activity Variance*)—of a neuron i:

$$VA_i \triangleq < \|y_i - \overline{y_i}\|^2 >, \tag{2.6}$$

where y_i is the output activation level for neuron i, $\overline{y_i}$ is the average of y_i.

Using (2.4), we can define the operational measure of VA_i as

$$\widehat{VA_i}[n] \triangleq \gamma_v \widehat{VA_i}[n-1] + (1 - \gamma_v)\|y_i - \widehat{Act_i}[n]\|^2, \tag{2.7}$$

where

$$\widehat{Act_i}[n] \triangleq \gamma_a \widehat{Act_i}[n-1] + (1 - \gamma_a)y_i[n] \tag{2.8}$$

is the operational measure of the average output activity for neuron i.

VA_i is very closely related to the information content (or entropy, in the terminology of information theory) of the output signals of neuron i. Zero VA_i for a given neuron i means that no information is generated by this neuron; hence this neuron is not performing any signal processing function and can be eliminated from the network.

To annihilate a neuron according to the second criterion in Guideline 2.3, we need to identify the redundancy in the network. This can be done by watching the dependency between the output values of neurons in the network. If two neurons are totally dependent, (which means that given the output value of one neuron, the output of the other neuron can be decided with probability one), then one of the neurons can be annihilated without affecting the performance of the network. A sufficient condition for two neurons to be highly dependent is that the values of their parameter structure are very similar to each other. In the simple neuron case (i.e, neurons without internal function tree structure), the situation stated above corresponds to the closeness of the weight vectors of the two neurons. Hence if we monitor the similarity between the input weight vectors of neurons in the network and whenever the weight vectors of two neurons are "very close" to each other, then one of them can be eliminated. Exactly how close is "very close" would be problem dependent and is also related to the resource constraint of the physical implementations.

To identify the closeness between the input weight vectors of two neurons is a fairly easy job for topological neural networks (like the SPAN network in Chapter 4) and only requires local operations; however it would require us to search through a substantial subset of the neurons in the neural networks without topological relationships between neurons (like multi-layer feed-forward networks).

2.5.3 Structural Relationship Modification

Following similar procedure as the one we use to define neuron generation/annihilation processes, we can define the firing criteria for other structure level adaptation operators. In particular, we want to define the criteria to modify the structural relationship between neurons in the network for a given P-Level network model. These criteria are model dependent because the structural relationships between neurons are different among different models. However, the activity-based approach introduced in this chapter can still be used. Here we first need to define the structural relations in the network as objects, just as we defined the ICM and OCM in the formal neuron model; then, based on the activities of those relational objects and the attribute objects of those relations, we can define the firing criteria of the structure operators for any specific neural network model. Chapter 4 offers examples of this class of operators.

2.6 Summary

The general framework outlined in this chapter allows us to specify a very broad spectrum of neural networks, in particular, the advantages are summarized in the following:

- The idea of parameterized function tree F allows the neural network to have a wider range of association power than the traditional inner product type of dendrite models. The following are some possibilities:

  - High order association between neurons can be modeled by using polynomial functions in F.

- By using delay functions in F, a neuron can have the ability to associate temporal signals.

- The idea of specifying neural networks hierarchically is useful for designing and implementing large network structures.

- The idea of putting neural networks in a topological space is important for the S-Level adaptation process, because the underlying topological space supports the neural network with some spatial measure to guide the the network to adapt itself structurally. Actually, biological study of the nerve system development suggests that positional information is important to help the dendrite and axon tree to develop appropriate interconnection structures [55]. It was even proposed that the positional information plays a crucial role throughout the entire animal embryonic development process [31].

A good and complete formal model is useful for analysis, design, and implementation of any engineering construct. This kind of formal structure is also important if we want to manipulate the structure of artificial neural networks, because before we can actually do useful processing on an object, we must be able to specify it clearly enough. This is the reason why I adopt such a formal approach in this definition chapter. In later chapters, I will apply the basic formalism presented in this chapter to define two S-Level neural networks.

Chapter 3

Multi-Layer Feed-Forward Networks

3.1 Introduction

Recent developments in neural network theory show that multi-layer feed-forward neural networks with one hidden layer of neurons can be used to approximate any multi-dimensional function to any desired accuracy, if a suitable number of neurons are included in the hidden layer and the correct interconnection weight values can be found [28].

Under a given structure, the appropriate interconnection weights can be found using the error back-propagation algorithm [108, 109]. However, adapting the interconnection weights only partially solves the problem, because the correct functional representation in this kind of network requires finding both the correct weights and a suitable number of neurons in the hidden layers. Even if the system designer can successfully figure out the structure of the network in the beginning, later on, if the statistics or the characteristics of the problem change, the originally designed network structure might not be able to represent the problem and to generate the desired response through adjusting the weights.

In this chapter, I address the idea of applying the structure level adaptation concept to feed-forward multi-layer neural networks [79]. The multi-level adaptation for multi-layer feed-forward neural networks is first formulated under the basic formalism presented in Chapter 2. A structure level feed-forward network, **FUNNET (FUNction NET-work)** is defined. Then a flexible representation scheme for FUNNET is introduced. This data structure can support all the required structure level operations for FUNNET, and forms the basic framework for a software simulator. In the last part of this chapter, I will show a simple illustrative example together with computer simulation results to demonstrate the ideas introduced in this chapter.

3.2   Function Level Adaptation

The mathematical theories behind multi-layer feed-forward networks can be traced back to the so called "13th problem of Hilbert" [83], which was posed by Hilbert at the turn of this century, along with a series of difficult problems for 20th century mathematicians to think about. This problem was answered by Kolmogorov [69] in 1957 in the form of the famous Kolmogorov's Theorem. Recently, Cybento [28] showed that it is possible to approximate any multi-dimensional function to any desirable degree of accuracy simply by superposition of a sigmoidal function. The relevant mathematical theorems are summarized in Appendix A.

Figure 3.1 shows the general schematic diagram of a multi-layer feed-forward neural network. The neurons in this network are arranged in layers. The *receptive field* of each neuron in the network contains all the neurons in the previous layer, and the *projective field* of each neuron

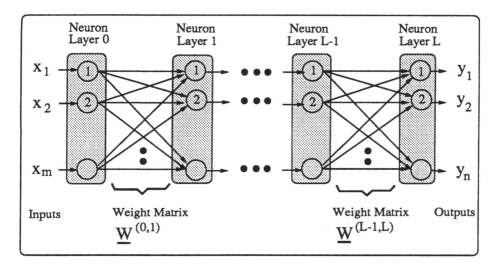

Figure 3.1: A Multi-layer feed forward neural network.

contains all the neurons in the next layer. The interconnection weights between neurons in two adjacent layers $l - 1$ and l are specified by the weight matrix $\underline{\mathbf{W}}^{l-1,l}$. The ith row of $\underline{\mathbf{W}}^{l-1,l}$ corresponds to the input weight vector for the ith neuron in layer l. The I-Set of the network contains all the neurons in the first layer (corresponding to layer 0 in Figure 3.1) and the O-Set of the network contains all the neurons in the last layer (corresponding to layer L in Figure 3.1). The function of this kind of network is to form a multi-dimensional mapping between the input space (in Figure 3.1, R^m) and the output space (in Figure 3.1, R^n). Each neuron in the network (designated by the circles in Figure 3.1) performs a summing and thresholding function of the following form:

$$q_i^{(l)} = \sigma\left(\sum_{j=1}^{K_{l-1}} w_{ij}^{(l-1,l)} q_j^{(l-1)} - \theta_i^{(l)}\right) \tag{3.1}$$

where $q_i^{(l)}$ designate the output of the ith neuron in the l th layer, $w_{ij}^{(l-1,l)}$ is the interconnection weight between the ith neuron in layer l and the

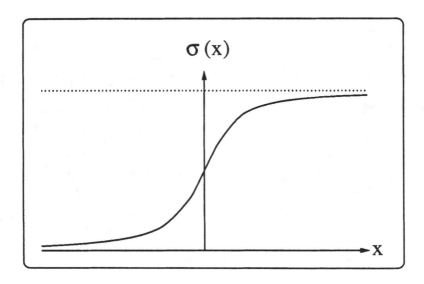

Figure 3.2: A typical sigmoidal function.

jth neuron in layer $l-1$, $\theta_i^{(l)}$ is the threshold for the ith neuron in layer l, K_{l-1} is the number of neurons in layer $l-1$, and $\sigma()$ is the sigmoidal function. In most of the current neural network literature, sigmoid is a monotonic increasing function bounded above and below between two finite extreme values. Figure 3.2 shows the form of a typical sigmoidal function. The most commonly used sigmoidal function, which is the same as the "Fermi Distribution" used in statistic mechanics, is shown in the following:.

$$\sigma(x) = \frac{1}{1 + e^{-x/T}}, \tag{3.2}$$

where T, called the temperature, is a factor used to control the steepness of the sigmoidal function. The smaller T, the steeper is the slope of $\sigma()$. When $T \to 0$, $\sigma()$ becomes a step function.

As a matter of fact, the sigmoidal function does not need to be monotonic increasing as the one shown in equation (3.2). Cybento [28] showed that a three layer network with the sigmoidal function $\sigma(x)$ of neurons satisfying the following property is sufficient to form any given mapping (see Appendix A for the description of the theorem):

$$\sigma(x) \rightarrow \begin{cases} 1 & \text{as } t \rightarrow +\infty, \\ 0 & \text{as } t \rightarrow -\infty. \end{cases} \tag{3.3}$$

If we introduce a constant pseudo-neuron 0 in every layer with their output equal to -1, and let $w_{i0}^{(l-1,l)} = \theta_i^{(l)}$, then (3.1) can be rewritten as

$$q_i^{(l)} = \sigma\left(\sum_{j=0}^{K_{l-1}} w_{ij}^{(l-1,l)} q_j^{(l-1)}\right). \tag{3.4}$$

The function level dynamics of the network are activated by presenting an input vector $X = (x_1, x_2, \ldots, x_m)$ to the network. The neurons in layer 0 are the sensing neurons, which have outputs exactly the same as the input signals, i.e. $q_1^{(0)} = x_1$, $q_2^{(0)} = x_2$, etc. The function level adaptation is then carried out by changing the output of neurons in the network according to (3.1), starting from the neuron in the first layer. The output vector $Y = (y_1, y_2, \ldots, y_n)$ is composed of the outputs of the neurons in the last layer of the network, i.e. $y_1 = q_1^L$, $y_2 = q_2^L$, etc.

From Corollary 2.1 and 2.4, we know that this kind of network is state consistent; hence the outputs of the network can be derived from the inputs of the network at the same time index without causing state inconsistency.

3.3 Parameter Level Adaptation

After the output vector Y of the network is formed, it is compared with a desired output vector $\hat{Y}$ and the error vector $E = \hat{Y} - Y$ is calculated.

The parameter level adaptation of the network is done by adjusting the interconnection weights $\{w_{ij}^{(l)}\}$ and thresholds $\{\theta_i^{(l)}\}$ in the network toward the direction of minimizing the mean square error $\mathcal{E} \overset{\triangle}{=} < \|E\|^2 >$. The most well-known way of doing parameter adjustment in this class of networks is through the error back-propagation algorithm. Basically, the error back-propagation algorithm implements gradient descent of the form

$$\Delta w_{ij}^{(l-1,l)} = -\eta \frac{\partial \mathcal{E}}{\partial w_{ij}^{(l-1,l)}}, \tag{3.5}$$

where η, called *learning rate*, is used to control the convergent speed of the learning process. A larger η would make the learning speed faster, but is more likely to cause the system to become unstable. Hence the criterion for choosing an appropriate η is to find a suitable tradeoff between learning speed and stability.

Starting with neurons in the last layer, and by using the chain rule to calculate the gradient for the weights in the hidden layers, we can calculate all the $\Delta w_{ij}^{(l-1,l)}$ in equation (3.5) [108, 109]; the basic procedure is described in the following algorithm.

Algorithm 3.1 (Error Back-Propagation) :
At every time index n, starting from the output layer, for each layer l (other than the the input layer), and for each neuron j (other than the pseudo-neuron) in layer l, do the following steps:

1. *If l is the output layer, assign the* post-sigmoidal error $e_j^{(l)}[n]$ *as follows:*

$$e_j^{(l)}[n] \leftarrow \widehat{y}_j - y_j \tag{3.6}$$

Else:

$$e_j^{(l)}[n] \leftarrow \sum_{i=1}^{K_{l+1}} w_{ij}^{(l,l+1)} \delta_i^{(l+1)}[n], \qquad (3.7)$$

where index i runs through all the neurons in layer l + 1.

2. *Assign the* pre-sigmoidal error $\delta_j^{(l)}[n]$ *as follows:*

$$\delta_i^{(l)}[n] \leftarrow \sigma^{(1)}(p_i^{(l)}[n]) e_i^{(l)}[n] \qquad (3.8)$$

where $\sigma^{(1)}(p_i^{(l)}[n])$ is the first derivative of the sigmoidal function with net input $p_i^{(i)}[n]$, [1]

3. *Calculate the change of the weight between neuron j and every neuron k (including the pseudo-neuron) in layer l − 1 as follows:*

$$\Delta w_{jk}^{(l-1,l)}[n] \leftarrow \eta \delta_j^{(l)}[n] q_k^{(l-1)}[n] \qquad (3.10)$$

4. *Modify the weights:*

$$w_{jk}^{(l-1,l)}[n+1] = w_{jk}^{(l-1,l)}[n] + \Delta w_{jk}^{(l-1,l)}[n] \qquad (3.11)$$

◇

---

[1]The net input $p_i^{(l)}$ for the *i*th neuron in layer *l* is defined as

$$p_i^{(l)} \triangleq \sum_{j=0}^{K_{l-1}} w_{ij}^{(l-1,l)} q_j^{(l-1)} \qquad (3.9)$$

3.4   Structure Level Adaptation

In this section, I extend the multi-layer feed-forward network model to include structure level adaptation. This newly defined structure level neural network is called FUNNET (FUNction NETwork).

As suggested in Chapter 2, the first step to define an S-Net is to identify the E-space (Guideline 2.1). Because the purpose of the multi-level feed-forward neural network is to approximate some multi-dimensional functional mapping, the E-space $\mathcal{N}$ for an L layer FUNNET can be defined as the following for an $\mathcal{R}^n$ to $\mathcal{R}^m$ mapping:

$$\mathcal{N} = \{G|G \text{ is an } L \text{ layer } n \text{ input } m \text{ output } feed - forward \text{ } network\}.$$
$$(3.12)$$

The spanning operator set (SOS) Φ for the E-space $\mathcal{N}$ in (3.12) is composed of two kind of operators, $\Phi = \Phi_G \cup \Phi_A$:

$$\Phi_G = \{a^+(l)|1 \le l \le L - 1 \text{ is layer index}\} \qquad (3.13)$$

where $a^+(l)$ is the operator to generate a neuron in layer l; and

$$\Phi_A = \{a^-(l,i)|1 \le l \le L-1 \text{ is layer index}; i \text{ is neuron index}\}, \quad (3.14)$$

where $a^-(l,i)$ is the operator to remove neuron i from layer l.

Now the problem arises in determining the SEA (structure Evolution Automata) for FUNNET. Basically, this requires us to specify the rules for firing the two sets of operators defined above.

3.4.1   Neuron Generation

The situation for neuron generation is when the representation power of the network is insufficient. Cybento [28] showed that feed-forward neural networks with one hidden layer construct a class of functions which is dense in the space of continuous functions. This suggests that, given enough neurons in the hidden layer, a three layer network (consider the input also as a layer, as in Figure 3.1) can form any mapping to any desirable precision. Hence we can use the stabilized error as an index to determine whether the network needs to generate a new neuron. If after a certain period of parameter adaptation, the error is stablized, but is larger than the desired value, then a new neuron can be generated.

If a neuron is to be generated, then the next question is where in the network to place the new neuron. The idea is to place it in the position where it is most needed [75, 77, 76]. This desirable position can be found through monitoring the learning behavior of the neurons in the network. More representation power is required for the neuron that contributes more to the final system error through the fluctuation in its input weight vector. This is because if a neuron has enough power to represent the region that it takes care of, then after a long time of parameter adaptation, its input weight vector should converge to a certain value and not fluctuate too much thereafter. On the other hand, if after a long period of parameter adaptation, the input weight vector of a neuron still fluctuates greatly, then this means that the neuron does not have enough representation power to learn the sub-problem that it is supposed to learn; hence the neuron can be split into two, i.e. we can add another neuron to the network with exactly the same interconnection as its parent neuron.

The above statement describes exactly what was formulated in Guideline 2.2 in Chapter 2. Now we need a suitable measure for Equation (2.5). To find the neuron which contributes most to the output distortion of the network, I define a measure $FD_i^{(l)}$ (called the *Fluctuated Distortion Measure (FD)*, see Appendix B for detailed derivation):

$$FD_i^{(l)} = |\delta_i^{(l)}| \, \|Q^{(l-1)}\| < \|\Delta W_i^{(l-1,l)}\| > \qquad (3.15)$$

where $\delta_i^{(l)}$ is the pre-sigmoidal error [2] for the ith neuron in layer l; $Q^{(l-1)}$ is the receptive field for the neurons in layer l, which is the vector formed by the output values of the neurons in the $l-1$th layer; $< \|\Delta W_i^{(l-1,l)}\| >$ is the average length of fluctuation of the input weight vector for neuron i in layer l. The Walking Distance (WD) defined in Chapter 2 (Equation (2.3)) can be used to dynamically measure $< \|\Delta W_i^{(l-1,l)}\| >$; hence we have the following operational measure for $FD_i^{(l)}$:

$$\widehat{FD}_i^{(l)}[n] = |\delta_i^{(l)}[n]| \, \|Q^{(l-1)}[n]\| \, \widehat{WD}_i^l[n]. \qquad (3.16)$$

The total increase in system distortion owing to the fluctuation of the neuron weight vectors can be measured by the following equation (see Appendix B for proof):

$$\Delta \mathcal{E}_W \propto \sum_{each\ neuron\ i\ and\ each\ layer\ l} \widehat{FD}_i^{(l)} \qquad (3.17)$$

Hence $\widehat{FD}_i^{(l)}$ is a measure of the contribution of neuron i in layer l to the total system distortion. The neuron with the highest $\widehat{FD}_i^{(l)}$ is selected to be split into two when neuron generation is required (not including the neurons in the input and output layers).

3.4.2 Neuron Annihilation

From Guideline 2.3, we know that under two circumstances, a neuron can be annihilated without affecting the performance of the network:

---

[2] $\delta_i^{(l)} \triangleq \sigma'(p_i^{(l)})e_i^{(l)}$, where $e_i^{(l)}$ is the post-sigmoidal error propagated to the ith neuron in layer l.

1. When the neuron is not a functioning element of the network, or

2. When the neuron is a redundant element of the network.

The first situation can be identified by checking the output information content of each neuron in the network. If the output entropy of a particular neuron is very close to zero (which means, that it is almost a constant), then the neuron can be annihilated without affecting the performance of the network. This low information condition can be monitored by examining the output fluctuation of each neuron in the network. If a neuron has an essentially constant output value, then it can be annihilated. The operation measure $\widehat{VA}_i[n]$ for the variance of output activity defined in Chapter 2 (Equation(2.7)) can be used for this purpose; here I measure the post-sigmoidal activity variation of each neuron i in layer l by the following equation:

$$\widehat{VA}_i^{(l)}[n] = \gamma_v \widehat{VA}_i^{(l)}[n-1] + (1 - \gamma_v)\|q_i^{(l)} - \widehat{Act}_i^{(l)}[n]\|^2, \qquad (3.18)$$

where

$$\widehat{Act}_i^{(l)}[n] = \gamma_a \widehat{Act}_i^{(l)}[n-1] + (1 - \gamma_a)q_i^{(l)}[n], \qquad (3.19)$$

As suggested in Chapter 2, the second situation can be identified by watching the dependency between the output values of neurons in the network. If two neurons are totally dependent, (which means given the output value of one neuron, the output of the other neuron can be decided with probability one), then one of the neurons can be annihilated without affecting the performance of the network. For feed-forward networks, a sufficient condition for two neurons to be totally dependent is that they have exactly the same receptive field and that their input weight vectors and thresholds determine the same hyperplane in the hyperspace spanned by their receptive field. This criterion can be checked by monitoring the input weight vectors (including threshold) of neurons in the same layer; if two of them are linear dependent, then they represent the same hyperplane and one neuron can be annihilated. However, since there are no topological relationships between neurons in the same layer (in contrast to topological neural networks, an example of which will appear in Chapter 4), checking the redundancy in a certain neuron layer would require comparing every pair of neurons within the layer; hence a computation complexity $O(N^2/L)$ is required for a N neuron network with L layers.

3.5   Implementation

A software simulation tool for FUNNET has been implemented. In this simulator, I use a doubly linked list to represent the dynamically adjustable structure.

Figure 3.3 shows the data structure used in the simulator. This data structure is very flexible and allows the following operations:

- Adding or killing neuron layers

- Generating or annihilating neurons within each layer

- Modifying the interconnection between neurons in two adjacent layers

Figure 3.4 shows the control flow chart of multi-level adaptation for multi-layer feed-forward neural networks. Phase 1 corresponds to the function level adaptation of this network and phase 2 corresponds to

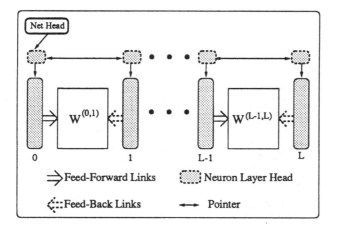

(a) Global structure

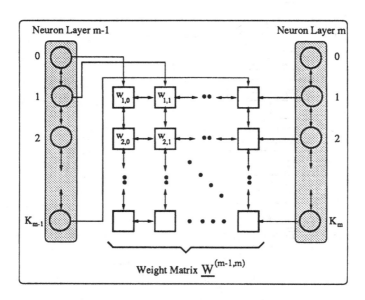

(b) Local structure between layers

Figure 3.3: The data structure for the FUNNET simulator. (a) The global structure, (b) The local structure between two adjacent layers. Neuron 0 in each layer is used to supply a constant and is called a pseudo-neuron.

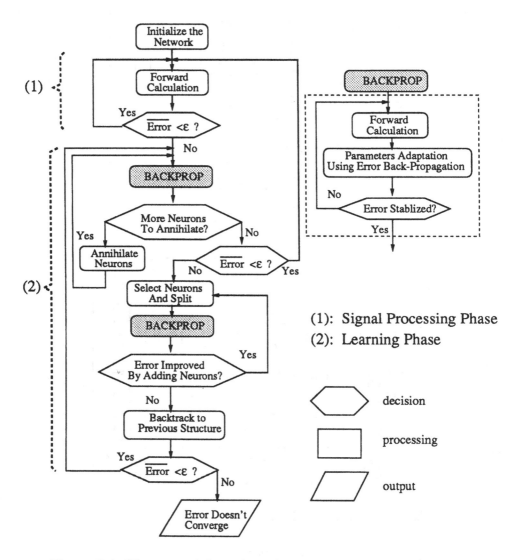

Figure 3.4: The control flow chart for the FUNNET simulator.

the parameter and structure level adaptation of the network. When the system converges into phase 1, it will remain there if the performance remains satisfactory. However, if the input statistics change and the error increases, then parameter or structure level adaptation will start again.

3.6 An Illustrative Example

In this section, I use a very simple example to demonstrate the ideas presented in the previous section. A 3-layer network initialized with two neurons in the hidden layer tests the structure level adaptation behavior for a problem with time varying statistics. The test problem is a two-class classification problem with 2-D input feature vectors. The time varying statistics of the test problem are shown in Figure 3.5. There are two output neurons in the network, with neuron 1 representing class 1 and neuron 2 representing class 2. The input vectors are randomly selected from the distribution regions of the two classes. When a pattern in a given class is presented, the neuron corresponding to that class should give a high output value and the other neuron should give a low output value.

This example uses the Fermi function (3.2) as the sigmoidal function. Figure 3.6 shows the learning curve for the adaptable structure network, where the magnitude of the output error is the error for the continuous threshold function ($T = 1$ in the sigmoidal function) and the mis-classification rate is the output error if the threshold function becomes a step function ($T = 0$ in the sigmoidal function). During period (a) in Figure 3.5, only two hyperplanes are needed to separate the decision regions; thus the two neurons in the initial configuration are sufficient and no neuron is generated. During period (b), class one becomes

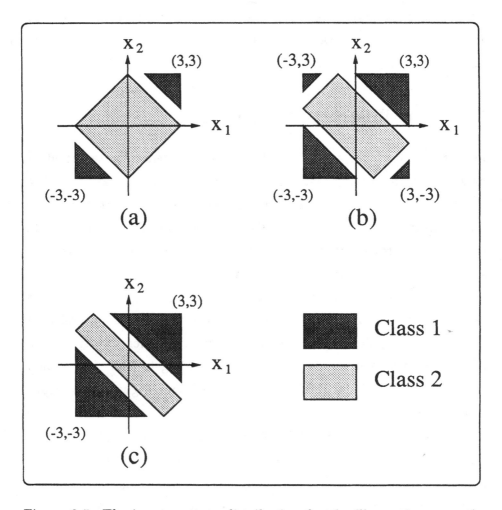

Figure 3.5: The input pattern distribution for the illustrative example (a) from iteration 0 to 1000; (b) from iteration 1001 to 5000; (c) from iteration 5001 to 7000.

four disconnected regions, and four neurons are needed; as a result, the network can find the desired number of neurons in the hidden layer and reduce the error to a minimum value. During period (c), class one again becomes two regions. Now because only two hidden layer neurons are needed, the network can annihilate the two unnecessary neurons and still keep very good performance.

As a comparison, I also simulate fixed structure networks with two internal neurons and four internal neurons; the learning curves are shown in Figure 3.7 and Figure 3.8 respectively. For the two neuron case, during period (b), the classification error cannot be eliminated because the network does not have enough neurons to represent the problem. For the four neuron case, during period (a) and (c), more neurons are required, which is a waste of resources.

Table 3.1 lists the convergent interconnection weights for the adjustable structure network at the end of each simulation period. It can easily be verified that the network has found the correct decision boundaries for all the three pattern distributions.

Table 3.2 and Table 3.3 show the interconnection weight values at the end of each period for the fixed structure cases with two neurons and four neurons respectively.

3.7 Summary

In this chapter, I introduced the structure level adaptation mechanisms of multi-layer feed-forward neural networks under the multi-level adaptation framework presented in Chapter 2, and demonstrated the operation of my proposed algorithm through a simple classification problem with time varying statistics. With the structure level adaptation added on top of the parameter adaptation for this kind of multi-level function network, the system will have complete adaptation power and potentially can be applied to problems that require finding a mapping between two multi-dimensional domains or general classification problems.

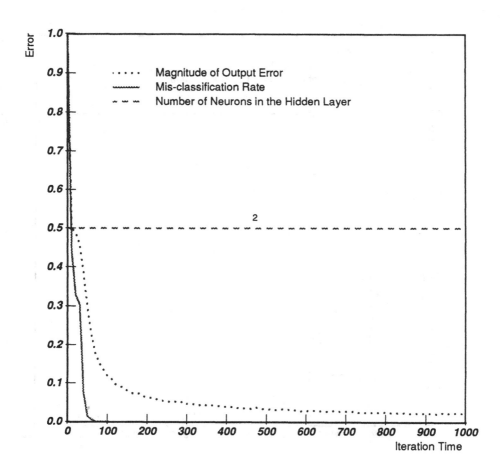

Figure 3.6: The error convergence behavior for the adaptable structure neural network.

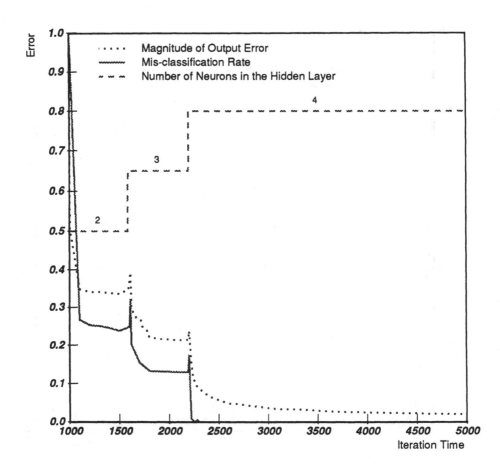

Figure 3.6, continued.

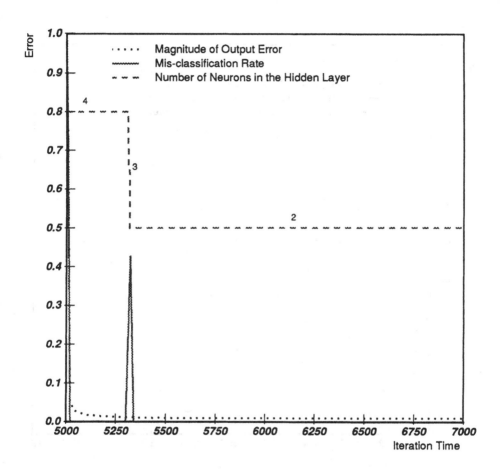

Figure 3.6, continued.

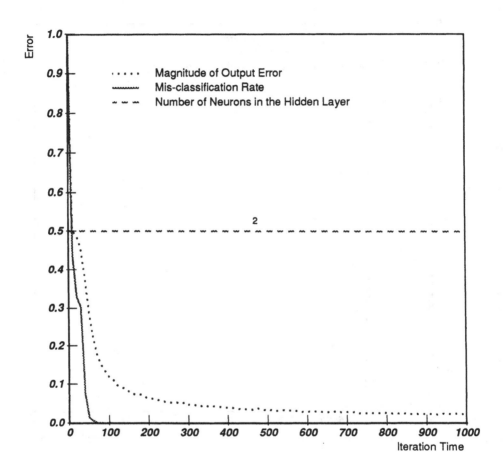

Figure 3.7: The error convergence behavior: 2 hidden layer neurons case.

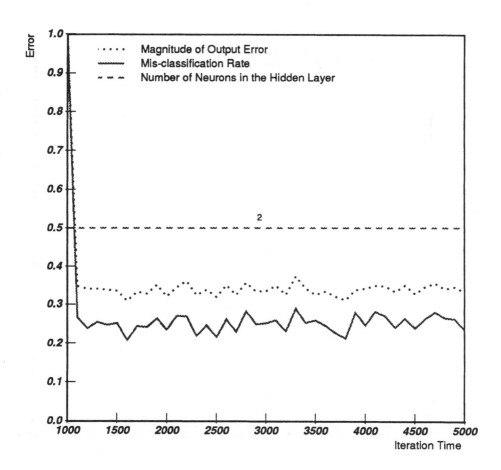

Figure 3.7, continued.

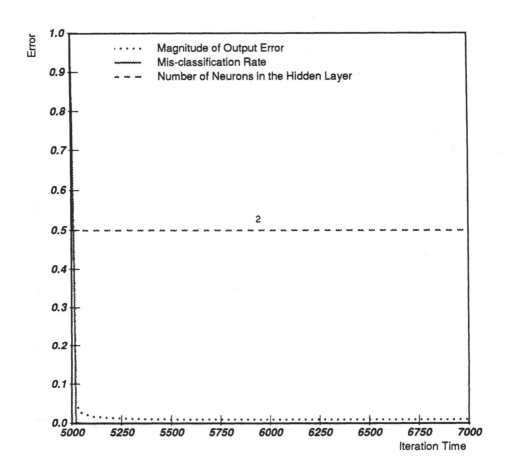

Figure 3.7, continued.

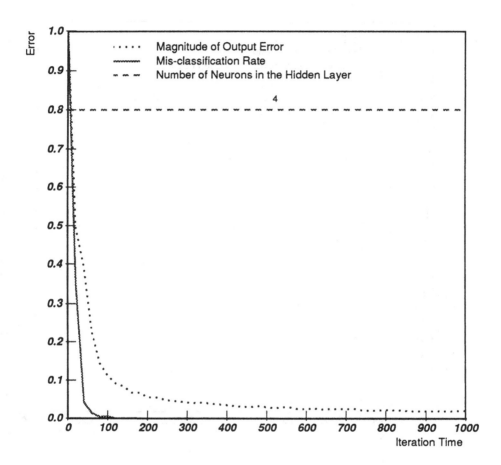

Figure 3.8: The error convergence behavior: 4 hidden layer neurons case.

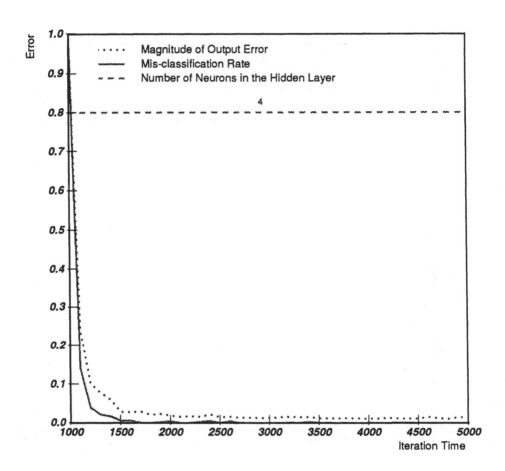

Figure 3.8, continued.

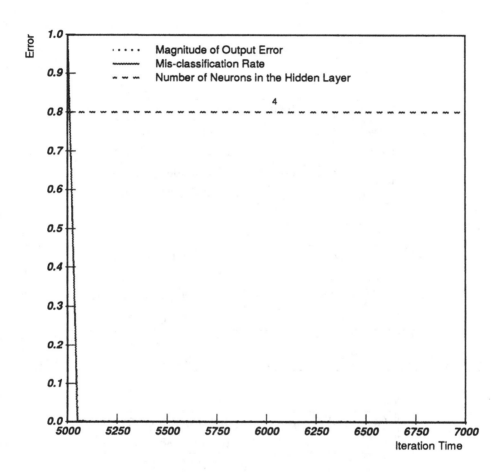

Figure 3.8, continued.

1000 iterations	
$(\mathbf{w}_{10}^{(0,1)}, \mathbf{w}_{11}^{(0,1)}, \mathbf{w}_{12}^{(0,1)})$	(9.044,2.671,2.675)
$(\mathbf{w}_{20}^{(0,1)}, \mathbf{w}_{21}^{(0,1)}, \mathbf{w}_{22}^{(0,1)})$	(-8.924,2.669,2.654)
$(\mathbf{w}_{10}^{(1,2)}, \mathbf{w}_{11}^{(1,2)}, \mathbf{w}_{12}^{(1,2)})$	(-4.559,9.306,-9.226)
$(\mathbf{w}_{20}^{(1,2)}, \mathbf{w}_{21}^{(1,2)}, \mathbf{w}_{22}^{(1,2)})$	(4.558,-9.306,9.335)

5000 iterations	
$(\mathbf{w}_{10}^{(0,1)}, \mathbf{w}_{11}^{(0,1)}, \mathbf{w}_{12}^{(0,1)})$	(11.103,4.469,4.469)
$(\mathbf{w}_{20}^{(0,1)}, \mathbf{w}_{21}^{(0,1)}, \mathbf{w}_{22}^{(0,1)})$	(-11.175,4.541,4.471)
$(\mathbf{w}_{30}^{(0,1)}, \mathbf{w}_{31}^{(0,1)}, \mathbf{w}_{32}^{(0,1)})$	(-13.051,2.981,-2.919)
$(\mathbf{w}_{40}^{(0,1)}, \mathbf{w}_{41}^{(0,1)}, \mathbf{w}_{42}^{(0,1)})$	(-12.792,-2.884,2.878)
$(\mathbf{w}_{10}^{(1,2)}, \mathbf{w}_{11}^{(1,2)}, \mathbf{w}_{12}^{(1,2)}, \mathbf{w}_{13}^{(1,2)}, \mathbf{w}_{14}^{(1,2)})$	(-14.784,9.570,-9.569,-10.194,-10.265)
$(\mathbf{w}_{20}^{(1,2)}, \mathbf{w}_{21}^{(1,2)}, \mathbf{w}_{22}^{(1,2)}, \mathbf{w}_{23}^{(1,2)}, \mathbf{w}_{24}^{(1,2)})$	(14.788,-9.572,9.572,10.197,10.268)

7000 iterations	
$(\mathbf{w}_{10}^{(0,1)}, \mathbf{w}_{11}^{(0,1)}, \mathbf{w}_{12}^{(0,1)})$	(10.087,5.663,5.623)
$(\mathbf{w}_{20}^{(0,1)}, \mathbf{w}_{21}^{(0,1)}, \mathbf{w}_{22}^{(0,1)})$	(-10.152,5.688,5.675)
$(\mathbf{w}_{10}^{(1,2)}, \mathbf{w}_{11}^{(1,2)}, \mathbf{w}_{12}^{(1,2)})$	(-7.733,13.276,-13.276)
$(\mathbf{w}_{20}^{(1,2)}, \mathbf{w}_{21}^{(1,2)}, \mathbf{w}_{22}^{(1,2)})$	(7.736,-13.279,13.279)

Table 3.1: The convergent neuron weight vectors for the adaptable structure neural network.

1000 iterations	
$(\mathbf{w}_{10}^{(0,1)}, \mathbf{w}_{11}^{(0,1)}, \mathbf{w}_{12}^{(0,1)})$	(9.044,2.671,2.675)
$(\mathbf{w}_{20}^{(0,1)}, \mathbf{w}_{21}^{(0,1)}, \mathbf{w}_{22}^{(0,1)})$	(-8.924,2.669,2.654)
$(\mathbf{w}_{10}^{(1,2)}, \mathbf{w}_{11}^{(1,2)}, \mathbf{w}_{12}^{(1,2)})$	(-4.559,9.306,-9.226)
$(\mathbf{w}_{20}^{(1,2)}, \mathbf{w}_{21}^{(1,2)}, \mathbf{w}_{22}^{(1,2)})$	(4.558,-9.306,9.335)

5000 iterations	
$(\mathbf{w}_{10}^{(0,1)}, \mathbf{w}_{11}^{(0,1)}, \mathbf{w}_{12}^{(0,1)})$	(15.867,5.169,5.138)
$(\mathbf{w}_{20}^{(0,1)}, \mathbf{w}_{21}^{(0,1)}, \mathbf{w}_{22}^{(0,1)})$	(-15.859,5.172,5.141)
$(\mathbf{w}_{10}^{(1,2)}, \mathbf{w}_{11}^{(1,2)}, \mathbf{w}_{12}^{(1,2)})$	(-7.331,8.092,-8.116)
$(\mathbf{w}_{20}^{(1,2)}, \mathbf{w}_{21}^{(1,2)}, \mathbf{w}_{22}^{(1,2)})$	(7.331,-8.092,8.116)

7000 iterations	
$(\mathbf{w}_{10}^{(0,1)}, \mathbf{w}_{11}^{(0,1)}, \mathbf{w}_{12}^{(0,1)})$	(13.760,7.505,7.479)
$(\mathbf{w}_{20}^{(0,1)}, \mathbf{w}_{21}^{(0,1)}, \mathbf{w}_{22}^{(0,1)})$	(-13.739,7.482,7.516)
$(\mathbf{w}_{10}^{(1,2)}, \mathbf{w}_{11}^{(1,2)}, \mathbf{w}_{12}^{(1,2)})$	(-5.056,9.498,-9.522)
$(\mathbf{w}_{20}^{(1,2)}, \mathbf{w}_{21}^{(1,2)}, \mathbf{w}_{22}^{(1,2)})$	(5.056,-9.498,9.522)

Table 3.2: The convergent neuron weight vectors for a fixed structure neural network: 2 hidden layer neurons case.

1000 iterations	
$(\mathbf{w}_{10}^{(0,1)}, \mathbf{w}_{11}^{(0,1)}, \mathbf{w}_{12}^{(0,1)})$	(5.178,3.850,1.200)
$(\mathbf{w}_{20}^{(0,1)}, \mathbf{w}_{21}^{(0,1)}, \mathbf{w}_{22}^{(0,1)})$	(-5.397,1.308,4.049)
$(\mathbf{w}_{30}^{(0,1)}, \mathbf{w}_{31}^{(0,1)}, \mathbf{w}_{32}^{(0,1)})$	(-5.272,-1.285,-3.987)
$(\mathbf{w}_{40}^{(0,1)}, \mathbf{w}_{41}^{(0,1)}, \mathbf{w}_{42}^{(0,1)})$	(5.244,-3.997,-1.274)
$(\mathbf{w}_{10}^{(1,2)}, \mathbf{w}_{11}^{(1,2)}, \mathbf{w}_{12}^{(1,2)}, \mathbf{w}_{13}^{(1,2)}, \mathbf{w}_{14}^{(1,2)})$	(-8.683,11.222,-10.980,-11.050,11.124)
$(\mathbf{w}_{20}^{(1,2)}, \mathbf{w}_{21}^{(1,2)}, \mathbf{w}_{22}^{(1,2)}, \mathbf{w}_{23}^{(1,2)}, \mathbf{w}_{24}^{(1,2)})$	(8.683,-11.221,10.979,11.049,-11.123)

5000 iterations	
$(\mathbf{w}_{10}^{(0,1)}, \mathbf{w}_{11}^{(0,1)}, \mathbf{w}_{12}^{(0,1)})$	(5.178,3.850,1.200)
$(\mathbf{w}_{20}^{(0,1)}, \mathbf{w}_{21}^{(0,1)}, \mathbf{w}_{22}^{(0,1)})$	(-5.397,1.308,4.049)
$(\mathbf{w}_{30}^{(0,1)}, \mathbf{w}_{31}^{(0,1)}, \mathbf{w}_{32}^{(0,1)})$	(-5.272,-1.285,-3.987)
$(\mathbf{w}_{40}^{(0,1)}, \mathbf{w}_{41}^{(0,1)}, \mathbf{w}_{42}^{(0,1)})$	(5.244,-3.997,-1.274)
$(\mathbf{w}_{10}^{(1,2)}, \mathbf{w}_{11}^{(1,2)}, \mathbf{w}_{12}^{(1,2)}, \mathbf{w}_{13}^{(1,2)}, \mathbf{w}_{14}^{(1,2)})$	(-8.683,11.222,-10.980,-11.050,11.124)
$(\mathbf{w}_{20}^{(1,2)}, \mathbf{w}_{21}^{(1,2)}, \mathbf{w}_{22}^{(1,2)}, \mathbf{w}_{23}^{(1,2)}, \mathbf{w}_{24}^{(1,2)})$	(8.683,-11.221,10.979,11.049,-11.123)

7000 iterations	
$(\mathbf{w}_{10}^{(0,1)}, \mathbf{w}_{11}^{(0,1)}, \mathbf{w}_{12}^{(0,1)})$	(4.665,3.693,2.713)
$(\mathbf{w}_{20}^{(0,1)}, \mathbf{w}_{21}^{(0,1)}, \mathbf{w}_{22}^{(0,1)})$	(-4.868,2.824,3.936)
$(\mathbf{w}_{30}^{(0,1)}, \mathbf{w}_{31}^{(0,1)}, \mathbf{w}_{32}^{(0,1)})$	(-4.809,-2.802,-3.782)
$(\mathbf{w}_{40}^{(0,1)}, \mathbf{w}_{41}^{(0,1)}, \mathbf{w}_{42}^{(0,1)})$	(4.648,-3.892,-2.791)
$(\mathbf{w}_{10}^{(1,2)}, \mathbf{w}_{11}^{(1,2)}, \mathbf{w}_{12}^{(1,2)}, \mathbf{w}_{13}^{(1,2)}, \mathbf{w}_{14}^{(1,2)})$	(-9.169,11.129,-10.882,-10.962,11.029)
$(\mathbf{w}_{20}^{(1,2)}, \mathbf{w}_{21}^{(1,2)}, \mathbf{w}_{22}^{(1,2)}, \mathbf{w}_{23}^{(1,2)}, \mathbf{w}_{24}^{(1,2)})$	(9.169,-11.128,10.881,10.960,-11.028)

Table 3.3: The convergent neuron weight vectors for a fixed structure neural network: 4 hidden layer neurons case.

Chapter 4

Competitive Signal Clustering Networks

4.1 Introduction

In this chapter, I apply the basic framework introduced in Chapter 2 to construct a multi-level competitive signal clustering network—SPAN. SPAN belongs to the category of *Lattice Neural Networks (LNN)* (see Definition 2.4 for the general definition), in which each neuron is assigned a position in a lattice. The lattice is useful for containing the information about the structural relation between neurons in the network. Through the competitive mechanisms between neurons in the network, the network can partition the input pattern space into regions and each region is assigned to a neuron which is most sensitive to that region. The neurons can also order themselves on the lattice in such a way that the structural relationships between regions in the pattern space are captured by the lattice structure.

This class of neural network is most useful for clustering unlabeled

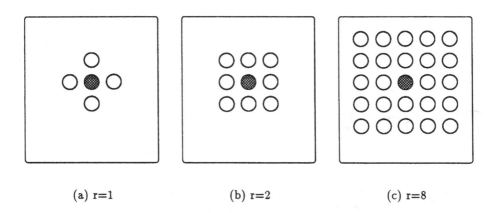

(a) r=1   (b) r=2   (c) r=8

Figure 4.1: Homogeneous neighborhood systems (HNS) (a) Minimum HNS, each neighborhood contains only the closest neighbors; (b) r=2 case, each neighborhood contains neighbors no farther than the 2nd closest neighbors; (c) r=8 case, each neighborhood contains neighbors no farther than the 5th closest neighbors.

signals to reduce information. The basic structures and mechanisms of SPAN are constructed according to the paradigm observed in the sensory cortex of most of the vertebrates [57, 58, 59] (Paradigm P.VIII in Figure 1.2).

4.2 Basic Structure

As indicated above, the neurons in SPAN are arranged in a lattice structure, with each neuron assigned a position in the lattice. In general, a k dimensional lattice $\mathcal{L}$ is defined as: $\mathcal{L} = \{\sum_{i=1}^{k} b_i \mathbf{v}_i \mid (b_1, b_2, \ldots, b_k) \in Z^n$, Z is the set of integers$\}$, where $\mathbf{v}_i, \mathbf{v}_2, \ldots, \mathbf{v}_k$ are a set of linearly independent vectors, called the *primitive translation vectors (PTVs)* of the lattice [62]. With PTVs defined, any point in the lattice can be represented by an index vector $(b_1, b_2, \ldots, b_k)$. In this chapter I will limit my discussion to only rectangular lattices [1]; however the ideas can be extended to more general lattices.

Each neuron i has a neighborhood $\mathcal{N}_i$, which is a set containing a group of neurons around i in the lattice. If $\mathcal{S}$ is the set of neurons and $\mathcal{N} = \{\mathcal{N}_i \mid i \in \mathcal{S}\}$ is the set of neuron neighborhoods, then the pair $\{\mathcal{S}, \mathcal{N}\}$ forms a graph in the usual sense. The neighborhood system used in this book belongs to the class of *Homogeneous Neighborhood Systems (HNS)*, defined in the following:

Definition 4.1 (HNS) : *A Homogeneous Neighborhood System (HNS) is of the form (see Figure 4.1):*

$$\mathcal{H} = \{\mathcal{H}_i \mid i \in S\}; \mathcal{H}_i = \{j \mid \|l_j - l_i\|^2 \leq r, j \in \mathcal{S}\} \qquad (4.1)$$

where $\mathcal{S}$ is the set of neurons, l_i and l_j are the lattice positions for neuron i and j respectively.

A HNS with $r = 1$ is called a Minimum Homogeneous Neighborhood System (MHNS). ◇

The input signals to the network are the source signals to be represented by the network. Each neuron in the network contains a group of variables, constituting the state of the neuron. Every neuron updates its state according to the input signals and the context of neuron states within its neighborhood. The state variables of each neuron can be categorized into three groups: Function level variables, Parameter level variables, and Structure level variables.

Notice that the general conceptual architecture of SPAN is similar to that of a *cellular automata* [139, 102, 100]. However, the difference

---

[1]In a rectangular lattice, the PTVs form an orthonormal set.

between SPAN and traditional cellular automata is that the structure of
SPAN is adaptable. SPAN can be considered the extension of a generalized version of Kohonen's *SOFM (Self-Organization Feature Map)* to
include structure level adaptation.

4.3   Function Level Adaptation

Figure 4.2 shows the function level signal flow diagram for a 1D SPAN.

There are two function-level variables (p_i, y_i) for each neuron i in
SPAN: where p_i is called the *pre-sigmoidal activation level* and y_i is
called the *post-sigmoidal activation level* or the *output level* for neuron i.

For neuron i, the rule for changing the pre-sigmoidal activation level
is

$$p_i[n] = a_1 F(Met(\mathbf{x}[n], \mathbf{w}_i)) + a_2 \sum_{j \in \mathcal{N}_i} y_j[n-1]\mu_{ij}, \qquad (4.2)$$

where $p_i[n]$ is the pre-sigmoidal activation level for neuron i at time
index n [2]; $\mathbf{x} = (x_1, x_2, \ldots, x_k)$ is the input vector of the network;
$\mathbf{w}_i = (w_{i1}, w_{i2}, \ldots, x_{ik})$, called the *input weight vector*, in which w_{ij},
called the *input interconnection weight* between input x_j and neuron i,
is the weight associating neuron i with input signal x_j; $F()$ is a positive
monotonic decreasing function, the purpose of which is to enable a neuron to generate a high output activation level when the input vector is
close to its weight vector in the pattern space; $Met()$ is a metric that
measures the distance between two vectors in a metric space. $\mathcal{N}_i$ is the
neighborhood set of neuron i; y_j is the output level of neuron j; and μ_{ij},
called the *lateral interconnection weight* between neuron j and neuron
i, is the weight associating neuron i with neuron j; μ_{ij} depends only

---

[2]In this book, we use $\xi[n]$ to denote the value of variable ξ at time index n.

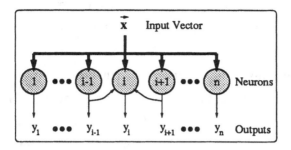

(a) Network Structure

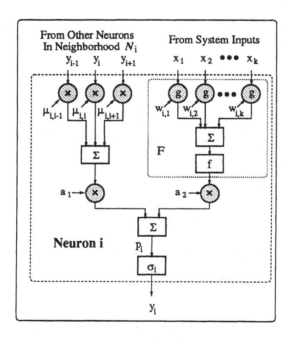

(b) Intra-Neuron Structure

Figure 4.2: The SPAN function level structure. (a) The network structure (A 1D case). (b) The intra-Neuron structure, where the shaded
circles represent the *modulating functions* and the boxes denote the node
functions in the function tree representation scheme introduced in Chapter 2.

on the relative position between neuron i and neuron j in the lattice, i.e. $\mu_{ij} = \eta(l_i - l_j)$, where l_i, l_j are the lattice indexes of neuron i and j respectively. $\eta()$, called the *spatial impulse response function* of the network, is normally in the form of a high pass filter (see Figure 4.3). This kind of lateral interconnection is very commonly seen in the visual systems in nature [27] and causes the output level of neurons to form clusters in the network for a given input signal. a_1 and a_2 in (4.2) are two constants used to weight the contribution of the system inputs and the outputs from other neurons to the activation level.

If we use a Euclidean metric for the $Met()$ in (4.2), then $F()$ can be written as (see Figure 4.2):

$$F(\mathbf{x}, \mathbf{w}_i) = f(\sum_{j=1}^{k} g(w_{ij}, x_j[n])); \tag{4.3}$$

$g()$ is a *Modulating Function (MF)* (see Chapter 2 for the general definition of a MF).

$$g(w_{ij}, x_j[n]) = (w_{ij} - x_j[n])^2,$$

and $f()$, which is a *Node Function (NF)* in the function tree of this neuron, can be defined as

$$f(z) = e^{-\lambda z},$$

The output level for neuron i is

$$y_i[n] = \sigma_i(p_i[n]), \tag{4.4}$$

where $\sigma_i()$ is the output function for neuron i. σ_i is of the same form as the sigmoidal function shown in Chapter 3 (Figure 3.2).

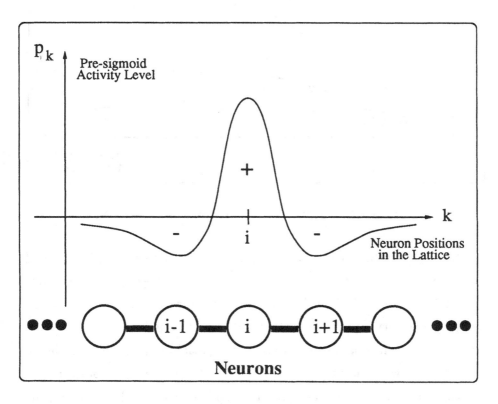

Figure 4.3: The spatial impulse response of SPAN. The distribution of neuron pre-sigmoidal activity level in a 1-D neuron array when neuron i is activated by an impulse. The negative part of the function represents lateral inhibition (i.e., negative interconnection weight).

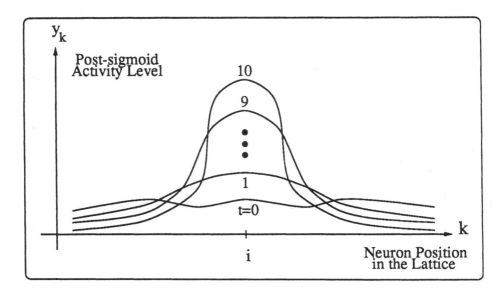

Figure 4.4: Output activity building up in SPAN.

Normally, in SPAN the input weight vectors of neurons are arranged in a topological order on the lattice, i.e., the input weight vectors vary smoothly across the network. This phenomenon is fairly commonly observed in sensory systems in nature [59, 111, 130, 96].

The lateral feedbacks weighted by the spatial filter of the form shown in Figure 4.3 will cause the network to form "center-around" output level distributions; i.e., after presenting the input signals to the network, the neuron output activity will gradually build up around some activity center in the network. Figure 4.4 shows a typical example of the dynamics of neuron outputs in SPAN.

Basically, by using this kind of lateral interconnection scheme, for any given initial random distribution of neuron activity level (assumed to be small) in the network, after presenting an input pattern [3], the system

---

[3]At the beginning of each relaxation process, the input pattern is presented to the network, and then removed; the relaxation process continues after removing the input

can reach a stable state within a small number of relaxation steps. After the stable state is reached, the neuron with the input weight vector most similar to the input pattern (i.e., the weight vector that maximizes the function $F()$ in (4.2)) will display the highest output level and the activity of most of the other neurons will be suppressed. The above process implements a fast pattern matching method using a relaxation method. The most attractive feature of this process is that the number of relaxation steps tends to be independent of the size of the network.

4.4 Parameter Level Adaptation

I follow Kohonen's learning algorithm [65, 66, 68] to adjust the input weight vectors of neurons in the network:

Algorithm 4.1 :

> **for** *(each time index n)* **do**
> > *fetch source signal* $\mathbf{x}[n]$
> > *select i:* $\|\mathbf{x}[n] - \mathbf{w}_i[n-1]\| \leq \|\mathbf{x}[n] - \mathbf{w}_k[n-1]\|, \forall k \in \mathcal{S}$
> > **for** *(∀j ∈ $\mathcal{N}_i$)* **do**
> > > $$\mathbf{w}_j[n] = \mathbf{w}_j[n-1] + \alpha\phi[n-1](\|\mathbf{l}_j - \mathbf{l}_i\|)(\mathbf{x}[n] - \mathbf{w}_j[n-1])$$
> > **end**
> **end**

◇

where $\mathbf{x}[n]$ is the input source signal of the network at time n; $\mathbf{w}_j[n]$ is the input weight vector of neuron j at time index n; $\mathcal{S}$ is the set of

---

pattern until the output level of neurons converges to a stable spatial distribution across the network.

neurons; α, called the *learning rate*, is a constant used to control the rate of convergence in the learning process; l_i is the position of neuron i in the lattice, and $\phi[n](d)$, called *spatial mask*, is a time varying function used to control the range of influence of a neuron to other neurons in the lattice. Kohonen [66] showed that if $\phi[\,](\,)$ is selected in such a way that the influence range is wide in the beginning and gradually decreases to a minimum value close to the end of the training process, then both fast convergence and final representation accuracy can be achieved.

The $\phi[\,](\,)$ used by Kohonen is

$$\phi[n](a) = \begin{cases} 1 & \text{if } a \leq R[n] \\ 0 & \text{otherwise,} \end{cases} \tag{4.5}$$

where $R[\,]$ is a positive definite monotonic decreasing function; the minimum value for $R[\,]$ is 1 for the network to retain organizing capability. In general, $\phi[n](\,)$ can be of the form

$$\phi[n](a) = \begin{cases} g(a/d[n]) & \text{if } a \leq R[n] \\ 0 & \text{otherwise,} \end{cases} \tag{4.6}$$

where both $g()$ and $d[\,]$ are positive definite monotonic decreasing functions. Notice that $R[n]$ in (4.6) and (4.5) defines a time varying HNS with the size of neighborhoods decreasing with time.

Kohonen's learning algorithm creates a topological, neighboring-relationship-preserving vector quantizer. After enough input training vectors have been presented, the input weight vectors of neurons will specify clusters or vector centers that sample the input space such that the point density function of the vector centers follows the probability density function of the input vectors in a certain functional form. In addition, the weights will be organized such that neighboring neurons on the network tend to have similar input weight vectors, that represent neighboring regions in the input pattern space. In particular, it can be shown that the asymptotic values of the weight vectors will tend to be the weighted centroid of their influence regions. The influence region for neuron i is the region Ω_i in the input pattern space, such that during the training process, whenever an input pattern falls in Ω_i, $\mathbf{w}_i$ will be modified. To be more specific, $\Omega_i = \bigcup_{j \in \mathcal{N}_i} V_j$, where V_j is the Voronoi region [4] for neuron j.

This idea is formalized in the following theorem (see Appendix C for the proof of this theorem).

Theorem 4.1 (Asymptotic Value of $\mathbf{w}_i$) :
Let $y_i(\mathbf{x}) = \phi(\|\mathbf{l}_i - C(\mathbf{x})\|)$, where $\mathbf{l}_i$ is the lattice position for neuron i and $C(\mathbf{x}) = \mathbf{l}_j$ is the lattice position for neuron j that has the input weight vector closest to the input signal $\mathbf{x}$. For sufficiently small learning rate α, the asymptotical value of weight vector for neuron i is

$$\widehat{\mathbf{w}}_i = \lim_{n \to \infty} \mathbf{w}_i[n] = \frac{\int_{\Omega_i} p(\mathbf{x}) y_i(\mathbf{x}) \mathbf{x} d\mathbf{x}}{\int_{\Omega_i} p(\mathbf{x}) y_i(\mathbf{x}) d\mathbf{x}} \qquad (4.7)$$

where $p(\mathbf{x})$ is the probability density function for input patterns. ◇

It can also be shown (see Appendix C) that the parameter level adaptation process defined in Algorithm 4.1 performs *gradient descent* on some energy surface defined for each individual neuron and the asymptotic weight vector, $\widehat{\mathbf{w}}_i$, minimizes the energy function for neuron i.

The properties stated in Theorem 4.1 make the network capable of catching the local context of incoming source vectors; thus suggesting that the network can be used for the following purposes:

---

[4]The Voronoi region V_j is the set of points which are closer to $\mathbf{w}_j$ than any other $\mathbf{w}_k$ in the pattern space.

- As an associative memory to restore the original signals from incomplete or degraded input patterns [66].

- As a sequence classifier to detect the patterns buried in the context of a sequence of input vectors [67, 128].

- As a context-sensitive VQ to eliminate the correlation between adjacent vectors in the input source signal streams. I will explore this idea further in Chapter 5.

4.5 Structure Level Adaptation

Basically, SPAN can be considered an S-Level network which is constructed based on a generalized self-organization feature map, defined in the following:

Definition 4.2 (Generalized SOFM) :
An n-dimensional **generalized SOFM (G-SOFM)** *with a k-dimensional input pattern space is specified by a pair* $T = < G, M_{\mathcal{H}} >$, *where* G = $\{N_1, N_2, \ldots\}$ *is a set of neurons with each* $N_i \in G$ *specified by the 4-tuple,* $< \sigma, (p_i, y_i), \mathbf{w}_i, \delta >$. *The F-Level dynamics of* N_i *are determined by the state transition function* σ *with*

$$y_i[* + 1] = \sigma(p_i[* + 1]),$$

where $p_i[* + 1]$ *is calculated according to equation (4.2).*

The P-Level dynamics of N_i *are determined by the parameter adjusting function* δ *with*

$$\mathbf{w}_i[* + 1] = \delta(\mathbf{w}_i[*], \mathbf{x}[* + 1]) = \mathbf{w}_i[*] + \alpha\phi[*](\|\mathbf{l}_s - \mathbf{l}_i\|)(\mathbf{x}[* + 1] - \mathbf{w}_i[*]),$$

where s is the selected neuron (based on the criterion which minizes the Euclidean distance between the input pattern and the weight vector of neurons) in the current training cycle.

$M_{\mathcal{H}} = (\mathbf{l}_1, \mathbf{l}_2, \ldots, \mathbf{l}_m)$ *is a list of non-duplicated vectors, with each* $\mathbf{l}_i$ *in* $M_{\mathcal{H}}$ *representing the position of neuron i in the lattice,* $\mathbf{l}_i \in \mathcal{H}$, *where* $\mathcal{H} = \{(b_1, b_2, \ldots, b_n) \mid r_{l,1} \leq b_1 \leq r_{u,1}; r_{l,2} \leq b_2 \leq r_{u,2}; \ldots; r_{l,n} \leq b_n \leq r_{u,n}\}$ *is the lattice universe for this G-SOFM, where* $r_{l,i}$ *and* $r_{u,i}$ *specify the lower and upper bound of the lattice universe for the i'th dimension,* $r_{l,i}, r_{u,i} \in Z.$ [5] ◇

A G-SOFM with every lattice position occupied by a neuron becomes a SOFM; as a result, we can define the SOFM in terms of the G-SOFM as the following:

Definition 4.3 (SOFM) :
A G-SOFM becomes a SOFM, iff the following condition is applied to Definition 4.2:

$$\forall \mathbf{h} \in \mathcal{H} \; \exists \mathbf{l}_i (\mathbf{l}_i \; in \; M_{\mathcal{H}}) \wedge (\mathbf{h} = \mathbf{l}_i)$$

◇

The difference between the G-SOFM and the SOFM is that in a G-SOFM, not all the positions in the n-dimensional arrays need to be occupied by neurons. If the statistical distribution of input patterns in the input pattern space covers the volume of a strange shape, a G-SOFM would have better flexibilities than a SOFM to represent the whole range of pattern distribution.

Definition 4.4 (SPAN) :
An n-dimensional SPAN (Space PArtition Network) is an S-Level network, specified by a 4-tuple $E = \langle T, \Phi, \Theta, J \rangle$, *defined as follows:*

---

[5] Z is the set of integers.

$\mathcal{T} = <\mathcal{G}, \mathcal{M}_H>$ is an n-dimensional G-SOFM; the Neural Network Space of the E-space ($\overset{bigtriangleup}{=} <\mathcal{N}, \Delta>$) for E is $\mathcal{N}(\ni \mathcal{T})$, called the G-SOFM space, is a set of G-SOFMs, specified by [6]

$$\mathcal{N} = \{\mathcal{T} = <\mathcal{G}, \mathcal{M}_H> \mid \|\mathcal{G}\| \in Z^+; \mathcal{M}_H \in ((Z^n)^{\|\mathcal{G}\|} - Dup(Z^n, \|\mathcal{G}\|))\} \text{ [7]}$$

Δ is the set of allowed structure level operators. Φ is the spanning operator set for $\mathcal{N}$, $\Phi \subseteq \Delta$. Each operator in Φ maps a member in $\mathcal{N}$ to another member in $\mathcal{N}$. Φ is a cover operator set for $\mathcal{N}$, i.e. : [8]

$$\forall \mathcal{T}_i \in \mathcal{N} \; \forall \mathcal{T}_j \in \mathcal{N} \; \exists P \in \Phi^+(= \cup_{i=1}^{\infty}(\Phi)^i) \; \mathcal{T}_j = P(\mathcal{T}_i)$$

The S-Level dynamics is characterized by the Structure Evolution Automata (SEA) Θ, a mapping that does two things:

1. According to the current structure control state $J[*]$, it selects a list of operators from Φ and applies them on current G-SOFM, $\mathcal{T}[*]$, in order to generate the next G-SOFM, $\mathcal{T}[* + 1]$.

2. It generates the next structure control state $J[* + 1]$ according to the current parameter state $\mathbf{w}_i[*]$s of the neurons in $\mathcal{T}$, the current input pattern $\mathbf{x}[*]$, and the current structure control state $J[*]$.

$\diamondsuit$

Definition 4.4 sketches a general profile of SPAN. A more detailed description of SPAN lies in the specification of Φ, Θ and J. Φ contains three classes of basic operators:

1. **Neuron Generation Operator**: generates a new neuron and attaches it to the lattice.

---

[6] We use $\|\mathcal{G}\|$ to denote the number of elements in the set $\mathcal{G}$.

[7] $Dup(Z^n, \|\mathcal{G}\|) \overset{bigtrigangleup}{=} \underbrace{(v_n, v_n, \ldots, v_n)}_{}\|\mathcal{G}\|v_ns, v_n \in Z^n$ (duplicating the same vector v_n $\|\mathcal{G}\|$ times, $v_n \in Z^n$).

[8] This means that starting from any point $\mathcal{T}_i \in \mathcal{N}$, by repetitively applying operators in Φ to $\mathcal{T}_i$ can reach any point $\mathcal{T}_j \in \mathcal{N}$, see Chapter 2.

2. **Neuron Annihilator Operator:** deletes a neuron from the lattice.

3. **Neuron Structural Relation Operators:** adjusts the structural relations between neurons, including modifying the structure of the lattice or changing the positions of neurons in the lattice.

Through structure level adaptation, SPAN can dynamically modify *the frame* that neurons reside in, so that the structure of the network always reflects that of the input pattern space.

4.5.1 Neuron Generation Process

The set of neuron input weight vectors in SPAN can be considered a vector quantization of the input pattern space, such that each neuron i is used to represent a region V_i in which all the points are closer to $\mathbf{w}_i$ than the input weight vector of any other neuron. As for any vector quantizer, there is a trade-off between quantization error and representation complexity in SPAN. Since increasing the number of neurons in SPAN will decrease the quantization error (or distortion) of the network, we can use quantization error as a measure to determine when to generate new neurons. If a neuron i contributes too much to the average distortion of the network, then its Voronoi region [9] V_i in the input pattern space is underrepresented by neuron i; a new neuron should be generated to "share" some of the "representation load" of neuron i so that the average system distortion can be decreased.

---

[9] As suggested by the name SPAN (Space PArtition Network), the neuron input weight vectors partition the input pattern space into regions, called *Voronoi regions*, with each region represented by one neuron. All the points in a region are closer to the input weight vector of the corresponding neuron than any other neurons in the network.

The average system distortion is

$$
\begin{aligned}
D &= E[\,\|\mathbf{x} - Q(\mathbf{x})\|^2] \\
  &= \int_V \|\mathbf{x} - Q(\mathbf{x})\|^2 p(\mathbf{x})d\mathbf{x},
\end{aligned}
$$

(4.8)

where $V = \bigcup_{i \in S} V_i$ is the input vector space.

Whenever the source signal $\mathbf{x}$ falls into the Voronoi region V_i, neuron i is selected to represent the input signal, and the vector quantizer replaces $\mathbf{x}$ by $Q(\mathbf{x}) = \mathbf{w}_i$; hence we may write

$$
D = \sum_{i=1}^{M} \int_{V_i} \|\mathbf{x} - \mathbf{w}_i\|^2 p(\mathbf{x})d\mathbf{x},
$$

(4.9)

where M is the number of neurons in the network.

The probability of selecting neuron i is

$$
P_i = \int_{V_i} p(\mathbf{x})d\mathbf{x},
$$

(4.10)

equation (4.9) may then be replaced by

$$
\begin{aligned}
D &= \sum_{i=1}^{M} \left(\int_{V_i} \|\mathbf{x} - \mathbf{w}_i\|^2 \frac{p(\mathbf{x})}{P_i} d\mathbf{x} \right) P_i \\
  &= \sum_{i=1}^{M} E[\,\|\mathbf{x} - \mathbf{w}_i\|^2 \mid \mathbf{x} \; in \; V_i] P_i \\
  &= \sum_{i=1}^{M} d_i P_i,
\end{aligned}
$$

(4.11)

where d_i is the average distortion observed by neuron i.

From equation (4.11), we know that the contribution of neuron i to the overall system distortion is $d_i P_i$. This can be used as the measure to guide the neuron generation process. Our proposed criterion for neuron generation is the following:

Suppose the allowable average system distortion is ϵ_d; then neuron i should be split into two neurons if

$$d_i P_i > \frac{\epsilon_d}{M}. \tag{4.12}$$

Now the question becomes how to measure d_i and P_i dynamically. To handle this, I follow the averaging mechanism introduced in equation (2.4) in order to define an *operational measure* of d_i as

$$\widehat{d}_i[n_i^k] = \gamma_d \widehat{d}_i[n_i^{k-1}] + (1 - \gamma_d) \parallel \mathbf{x}[n_i^k] - \mathbf{w}_i[n_i^{k-1}] \parallel^2, \tag{4.13}$$

where n_i^k is the time index when neuron i is the kth time being selected; $\widehat{d}_i[m]$ is the distortion measure for neuron i at time index m; and γ_d, a factor between 0 and 1, is used to control the *effective temporal window size* for the averaging process. Notice that $\widehat{d}_i$ is updated only when neuron i is selected; between n_i^{k-1} and n_i^k, $\widehat{d}_i$ stays the same. Notice also that equation (4.13) defines a moving average filter with infinite window size [48]. The input signal to the filter is the process $D_i[k] = \parallel \mathbf{x}[n_i^k] - \mathbf{w}_i[n_i^{k-1}] \parallel^2$. This idea is justified by the following algebraic manipulation:

If we repeatedly apply equation (4.13) to substitute $\widehat{d}_i$ in the right hand side of (4.13), then $\widehat{d}_i[n_i^k]$ can be rewritten as

$$\begin{aligned}
\widehat{d}_i[n_i^k] &= (1 - \gamma_d)(\parallel \mathbf{x}[n_i^k] - \mathbf{w}_i[n_i^{k-1}] \parallel^2 + \gamma_d \parallel \mathbf{x}[n_i^{k-1}] - \mathbf{w}_i[n_i^{k-2}] \parallel^2 \\
&\quad + \ldots + \gamma_d^{k-1} \parallel \mathbf{x}[n_i^1] - \mathbf{w}_i[0] \parallel^2) \\
&= (1 - \gamma_d)(\sum_{j=0}^{k-1} \gamma_d^j \parallel \mathbf{x}[n_i^{k-j}] - \mathbf{w}_i[n_i^{k-j-1}] \parallel^2)
\end{aligned}$$

$$= (1 - \gamma_d^k) \frac{\sum_{j=0}^{k-1} \gamma_d^j \| \, \mathbf{x}[n_i^{k-j}] - \mathbf{w}_i[n_i^{k-j-1}] \, \|^2}{\sum_{j=0}^{k-1} \gamma_d^j} \tag{4.14}$$

Notice in (4.14), $\gamma_d^k \to 0$ for large k; hence $\hat{d}_i$ represents a weighted average of the distortion for neuron i. The weights $\{\gamma_d^j\}$ are set up in order to emphasize more recent distortion measures in the averaging process. Notice also by adjusting the value of γ_d, we can control the *temporal window size* in the averaging process. The closer γ_d is to 1, the wider the effective window size; hence more samples are taken into the averaging process. A rule of thumb for determining γ_d is given in Appendix D. Similarly to (4.13), we define the operational measure of P_i as

$$\hat{P}_i[n_i^k] = \gamma_p \hat{P}_i[n_i^{k-1}] + (1 - \gamma_p) \frac{1}{Int[n_i^k]}, \tag{4.15}$$

where

$$Int([n_i^k]) = n_i^k - n_i^{k-1}. \tag{4.16}$$

Every time a neuron i is selected, $\hat{d}_i$ and $\hat{P}_i$ are checked to see if (4.12) is satisfied; if so, then a new neuron is generated.

When generating a new neuron for the network, we need to answer the following question: where to put the newly generated neuron in the lattice? The guideline used is as follows:

Guideline 4.1 (Neuron Generation in SPAN) :

1. *Find* acceptable empty lattice sites *within the neighborhood region of the parent neuron and list them in order of preference.*

2. *If the list generated in Step 1 is not empty, place the new neuron on the position specified by the top entry of the list.*

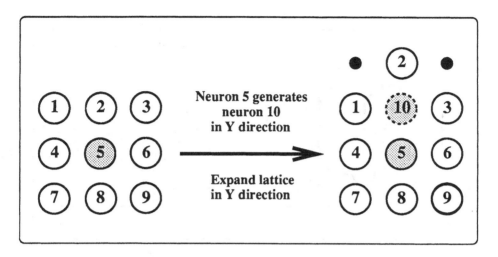

Figure 4.5: Lattice expansion. In this example, neuron 5 wants to generate a new neuron in the +Y direction, and since there is no empty site within the neighborhood of neuron 5, the lattice is expanded toward the +Y direction to accommodate the newly generated neuron 10.

3. *Else if the list is empty,* move the lattice *toward the* desirable direction *to make room for the new neuron (this operation is called* Lattice Expansion; *see Figure 4.5),*

◇

Since we want to preserve the structure of the input pattern space on the network, we must be careful about selecting lattice sites when generating new neurons. The criterion for selecting a new site is that it must be at a position that requires better representation power. This criterion can be evaluated based on the distribution of distortion on different *local lattice directions.* For each neuron i, we can define the local axes by looking into the context of neuron input weight vectors in the neighborhood of neuron i. For example, as shown in Figure 4.6, if

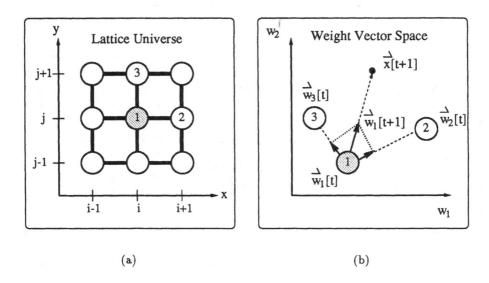

(a)   (b)

Figure 4.6: Local axes and the directional distribution of distortion.

neuron 2 is the closest neighbor of neuron 1 in the positive x direction on the lattice, then we can define the local $+x$ direction for neuron 1 as

$$\mathbf{x}_i^+ = \Lambda(\mathbf{w}_2 - \mathbf{w}_1), \qquad (4.17)$$

where $\Lambda()$ is the vector normalization operator, defined as follows:

$$\Lambda(\mathbf{y}) \stackrel{\triangle}{=} \frac{\mathbf{y}}{\|\mathbf{y}\|}. \qquad (4.18)$$

With the local axes defined for a given neuron, we can then define the distribution of average distortion on different local axes. For example, the average distortion on the $+x$ axis for neuron i can be defined as

$$\hat{d}_i.x^+[n_i^k] = \gamma_d \hat{d}_i.x^+[n_i^{k-1}] + (1 - \gamma_d)(r((\mathbf{x}[n_i^k] - \mathbf{w}_i[n_i^{k-1}]) \cdot \mathbf{x}_i^+))^2, \quad (4.19)$$

where $r()$ is the unit ramp function [10]; $\widehat{d}_i.x^-, \widehat{d}_i.y^+, \widehat{d}_i.y^-$ can be defined likewise.

Sometimes the local axis along a given direction can be inferred from other lattice directions even if the neighbors along that direction are missing. For example, if neuron i does not have $-x$ direction neighbors, but it does have $+x$ direction neighbors, then $\mathbf{x}_i^- \leftarrow -\mathbf{x}_i^+$ by inference.

Each neuron also keeps track of a measure called *alias energy*, which is the average distortion along the axes perpendicular to all the current axes. The operational measure of the alias energy of neuron i is the following:

$$\widehat{d}_i^\perp[n_i^k] = \gamma_d \widehat{d}_i^\perp[n_i^{k-1}] + (1 - \gamma_d) \|\mathbf{Proj}^\perp((\mathbf{x}[n_i^k] - \mathbf{w}_i[n_i^{k-1}]), i)\|^2, \quad (4.20)$$

where

$$\mathbf{Proj}^\perp(\mathbf{y}, i) \triangleq \mathbf{y} - \sum_j (\mathbf{y} \cdot \mathbf{a}_i^j)\mathbf{a}_i^j \quad (4.21)$$

is called the *alias operator*, which maps the vector $\mathbf{y}$ (in this case $\mathbf{x} - \mathbf{w}_i$) to its alias component related to all the local axes $\{\mathbf{a}_i^j\}$ of neuron i . $\widehat{d}_i^\perp$ is used as a measure to determine whether the current axes for neuron i are sufficient to represent the input patterns. If $\widehat{d}_i^\perp$ is high, a new axis must be generated. When a new axis is generated for neuron i, the new direction $\mathbf{a}_i^\perp$ is set to be $\Lambda(\mathbf{Proj}^\perp((\mathbf{x} - \mathbf{w}_i), i))$.

Whenever a new neuron is generated, its input weight vector is set to be

---

[10] A unit ramp function $r(x)$ is defined to be:

$$r(x) = \begin{cases} x & \text{if } x \geq 0 \\ 0 & \text{otherwise} \end{cases}$$

$$\mathbf{w}_{new} = \mathbf{w}_i + \delta\sqrt{\widehat{d_i}.a^j}\,\mathbf{a}_i^j, \tag{4.22}$$

where $\mathbf{a}_i^j$, the a^j axis for neuron i, is the local direction to put the new neuron; $\widehat{d_i}.a^j$ is the average distortion along axis a^j for neuron i; δ, a number between 0 and 1, is used to control the similarity between the newborn neuron and its parent.

4.5.2 Neuron Annihilation and Coalition Process

Following Guideline 2.3, we know that the number of neurons in SPAN must be decreased in two circumstances:

1. When a neuron is not *active* for a long period of time, or

2. WHen group of neurons are very similar to one another, such that all of them together over-represent the patterns in their Voronoi regions.

In the first case, the *virtually dead* neuron can be killed, because it is not contributing to the overall system output. An example of this case is when no input pattern falls into the Voronoi region of a neuron. The process of killing this neuron is called *neuron annihilation.*

To determine whether a neuron is active or not, I use the following neuron output activity measure defined in Chapter 2 (equation (2.8)), which is an operational measure of the average output activity of a neuron:

$$\widehat{Act_i}[n] = \gamma_a\widehat{Act_i}[n-1] + (1-\gamma_a)y_i[n],$$

where y_i is the output level for neuron i; in SPAN $y_i[n]$ is emulated by $\phi(\|C(\mathbf{x}[n]) - \mathbf{l}_i\|)$, where $C(\mathbf{x}[n])$ is the lattice position of the neuron which is the closest neighbor to the source signal $\mathbf{x}[n]$.

If after a long training period, $\widehat{Act}$ is very low for a particular neuron, then that neuron should be deleted. Similar to Equation(4.12), neuron i will be deleted if

$$\widehat{Act}_i < \frac{\epsilon_a}{M}.\qquad(4.23)$$

For the second case, if a set of neurons are very similar to each other, then the group of neurons must be merged to form a less populated group with the members in the new group inheriting the attributes from the members in the old one. The merge process can be performed pairwise, that is, checking the similarity between neighboring neuron pairs periodically; if their input weight vectors are too close, then one of the neurons can be eliminated, and the weight vector of the remaining neuron is set as the average of the two neurons. This process is called *neuron coalition.*

In both neuron annihilation and coalition, one neuron must be removed from the network. Before removing this neuron, a criterion must be satisfied: removing the neuron should not cause the graph $\{\mathcal{S},\mathcal{N}\}$ to become disconnected, where $\mathcal{S}$ is the set of neurons and $\mathcal{N}$ is the set of neighborhoods for the network. This criterion is a necessary condition for the network to retain self-organizing capability.

If deleting a neuron would empty a whole column or row in the lattice, then that column or row can be deleted; this operation is called *lattice shrinkage* (see Figure 4.7). The purpose of lattice shrinkage is to keep the representation simple and also to retain as much local interaction between neurons as possible. [11]

---

[11] The self-organizing ability of the network increases with the degree of local interaction between neurons. Lattice shrinkage may cause original non-interactive neurons to become neighbors, and hence would increase the degree of interactions in the network.

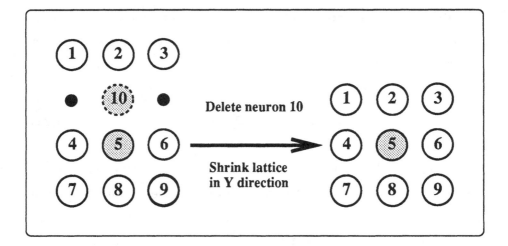

Figure 4.7: Lattice shrinkage. Neuron 10 is the last element in a row; after neuron 10 is killed, the whole row becomes empty. The row is then deleted to keep the representation minimum.

4.5.3   Structural Relation Adjustment

As the the statistics of the source signal evolve, the local dimensionality of a neuron might change. For example, as Figure 4.8 (a) shows, within the context of the neighborhood of neuron 2, the orientation of the $+y$ axis is very close to that of the $+x$ axis. If this happens, one of the neurons (in this case, neuron 3) should be moved to the local axis in which the other neuron resides (in this case, $+x$ axis), as depicted in Figure 4.8 (b). This process is called *axes merge*. Notice that after axes merge, the local dimensionality of neuron 2 decreases from 2 to 1.

The criterion for deciding when to make axes merge for a neuron i is to check the directional cosine between the relative input weight vectors from neuron i to the neighboring neurons. For example, if neuron j is a neighbor on the $+x$ axis and neuron k is a neighbor on the $+y$ axis of neuron i, then for every certain period of time, check

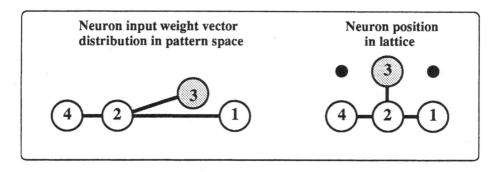

(a)

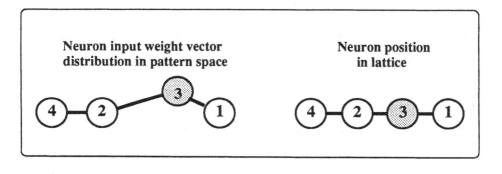

(b)

Figure 4.8: The axis merging process. (a) Neuron 1 and neuron 3 are the +X and the +Y direction neighbors of neuron 2 respectively. As the local +Y axis (defined by the relative weight vector between neuron 3 and neuron 2) approaches the +X axis (defined by the relative weight vector between neuron 1 and 2), the local dimensionality of the signal source distribution around neuron 2 decreases from 2 to 1. (b) Neuron 3 is merged to the X axis to reflect the change in local dimensionality.

$$\Theta_i^{+x,+y} = cos^{-1}(\Lambda(\mathbf{w}_j - \mathbf{w}_i) \cdot \Lambda(\mathbf{w}_k - \mathbf{w}_i)); \qquad (4.24)$$

if the value is too small, then one of the neighbors should be moved to the other axis.

In general, the criterion governing the axes merge process of neuron i is as follows: for every pair of local axes a^α, a^β on different dimensions [12], if there exist closest neighbors, neuron j and k, in both directions, then check

$$\Theta_i^{a^\alpha,a^\beta} = cos^{-1}(\Lambda(\mathbf{w}_j - \mathbf{w}_i) \cdot \Lambda(\mathbf{w}_k - \mathbf{w}_i)); \qquad (4.25)$$

if

$$\Theta_i^{a^\alpha,a^\beta} < \epsilon_\Theta, \qquad (4.26)$$

then one of the neighbors (in this case, neuron j or neuron k) should be moved to the other axis.

We can define other lattice structure modification operations for SPAN. For example, a neuron could jump to an empty site in its neighborhood if the context within the neighborhood of the new site is *better* than the old one as far as the weight vector of this neuron is concerned. I call this process *neuron migration*. Two neurons can also switch positions if better for both of them; this process is called *neuron swapping*. We can define a structural merit criterion, which is a function of the neuron weight vectors within the neighborhood of a neuron. This merit criterion can then be used as an energy function to guide the neuron migration and swapping processes. This merit criterion can be used to enforce several desirable features; among which are: more interaction between neighboring neurons, and local axes in good relative orientation (eg. x and y axes should be perpendicular to each other).

---

[12]Not all local axes are on different dimensions, e.g. $+x$ and $-x$ are on the same dimension.

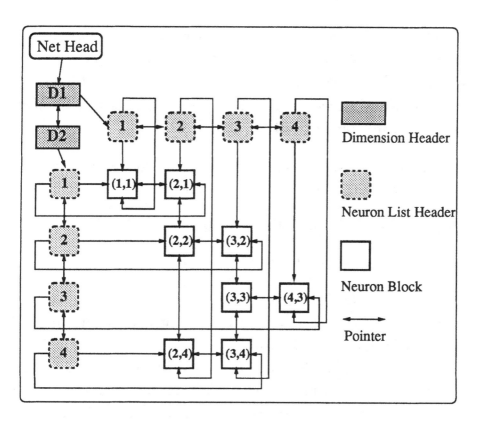

Figure 4.9: Doubly linked list representation of SPAN.

4.6   Implementation

A simulation tool for SPAN is implemented using a doubly linked list [78]. Figure 4.9 shows the representation of a 2D SPAN under the proposed doubly linked list structure. Under this representation structure, Each *neuron block* contains the information needed to specify a particular neuron (corresponding to the formal neuron defined in Chapter 2). The *neuron list header* points to a neuron list in a certain direction in the lattice. The neuron list headers for the same direction are also linked together as a list, called the *neuron list header list*. Each dimension header points to the *neuron header list* for a certain direction. For example, the dimension header D1 in Figure 4.9 points to the list of vertical neuron list headers and D2 points to the list of horizontal neuron list headers.

The structure shown in Figure 4.9 is very flexible and can support the following structural operations:

- Changing the structure of the lattice: including changing lattice dimension, changing the lattice size, etc.

- Generating and annihilating neurons

- Moveing neurons in the lattice

The firing rule for each of the structure level operators can be checked periodically [13]; whenever the firing criteria for an operator are satisfied, a structural operation is activated.

Algorithm 4.2 shows fragments of the procedure used in the SPAN simulator. Other structure level operators can be included in a the similar way as the generation and annihilation modules shown in Algorithm. 4.2.

---

[13]We do not need to do this kind of checking for every parameter adaptation cycle, because the structure evolution automaton (SEA) operates based on the statistics of the parameter level processes. If the P-Level statistics are very slow time varying, then the S-Level dynamics can be very slow and it is allowable to execute one structure level operation after many parameter level adaptation steps. This way the overhead in doing structure level adaptation can be minimized.

Algorithm 4.2 :

```
for (n = 1 to T_tr ) {
    generate one training pattern x ;
    function and parameter level adaptation ;
    ⋮
    if ((n mod M_anni) = 0) {
        for (each neuron m in the network) {
            if (Âct_m ≤ Θ_NA) {
                delete neuron m from lattice ;
                update lattice structure ;
            }
        }
    }
    if ((n mod M_gen) = 0) {
        for (∀j, φ[n](|l_j − l_i|) ≠ 0) {
            if (P̂_j ŴD_j ≥ Θ_NG) {
                if (no acceptable lattice site)
                    expand lattice L toward DHA_j ;
                choose h: (h − l_j) is DHA_j ;
                put new neuron on lattice position h ;
            }
        }
    }
    ⋮
}
```

where T_{tr} is the training time; $\widehat{WD}_j$ is the walking distance for neuron j; $\widehat{P}_j$ is the operational measure for the selection probability of neuron j; DHA_j is the direction of high activity for neuron j, which is the direction

that has the highest projected weight vector movement (see Figure 4.6);
$\widehat{Act}_j$ *is the activity measure; l_i is the lattice position of neuron i.*   ◇

4.7   Simulation Results

In this section, I will show the network evolution process of a simple test example to demonstrate the ideas presented so far.

The network in this example is a 2D SPAN with a MHNS (minimum homogeneous neighborhood system) [14]. The input pattern space is also two-dimensional. I will show the network evolution process for two test cases.

Case 1

The signal in the x_1 direction (corresponding to the w_1 direction of the neuron input weight vector) is uniformly distributed between 0.0 and 10.0. The signal in the x_2 direction (corresponding to the w_2 direction of the neuron input weight vector) gradually increases in distribution range and is uniformly distributed within that range. The following table summarizes the time varying statistics of the input pattern distribution:

Time Frame	Iteration range	x_1 range	x_2 range
1	1 → 5000	$0.0 \le x_1 \le 10.0$	$5.0 \le x_2 \le 5.0$
2	5001 → 15000	$0.0 \le x_1 \le 10.0$	$4.0 \le x_2 \le 6.0$
3	15001 → 25000	$0.0 \le x_1 \le 10.0$	$3.0 \le x_2 \le 7.0$
4	25001 → 290000	$0.0 \le x_1 \le 10.0$	$0.0 \le x_2 \le 10.0$

The lattice is initialized with one neuron. The neuron generating threshold ϵ_d is set to be 0.25 in this case.

---

[14] A minimum homogeneous neighborhood system (MHNS) is a HNS with $r = 1$, see Figure 4.1.

Figure 4.10 shows the distribution of neuron input weight vectors in the source signal space and the lattice structure during the network evolution process. In each graph, the circles represent neurons and the number inside each circle is the neuron ID. Neuron IDs are ordered according to the sequence of generation.

Initially, the source signals are distributed along one dimension (time frame 1); the lattice also grows along only one dimension. Notice also that the neuron sequence in the lattice preserves the order of neuron input weight vectors in the pattern space. Later on, as the range of the signal distribution in the x_2 direction is turning wide, neurons start growing on the second lattice dimension to follow the change in input pattern space. Finally, as the source signal distribution starts to cover the region $(0,0) \leq (x_1, x_2) \leq (10, 10)$, the network structure also grows to be a perfect rectangle lattice to cover the whole signal distribution range.

Case 2

The network is initialized with the final configuration of Case 1, i.e. 100 neurons arranged in a 10×10 lattice with their weight vectors distributed evenly in the range $(0,0) \leq (w_1, w_2) \leq (10, 10)$.

The time varying statistics of the signal source follow the reverse path as Case 1, that is, x_1 distribution spans the whole range and x_2 distribution shrinks to zero size. The following table summarizes the time varying statistics of the source signals:

Frame No	Iteration range	x_1 range	x_2 range
1	1 → 50000	$0.0 \leq x_1 \leq 10.0$	$1.0 \leq x_2 \leq 9.0$
2	50001 → 250000	$0.0 \leq x_1 \leq 10.0$	$5.0 \leq x_2 \leq 5.0$

Figure 4.11 shows the network reduction process for this case. As

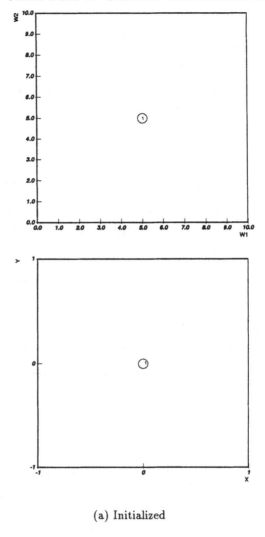

(a) Initialized

Figure 4.10: An example showing the network growing process. Each graph on the upper row displays the distribution of neuron weight vectors in the source signal space and each graph on the lower row shows the lattice structure of the network. The circles in each graph represent neurons and the number inside each circle is the neuron ID which is ordered in the sequence of generation. Each pair of neighboring neurons is connected by a bar. We have a MHNS is this example.

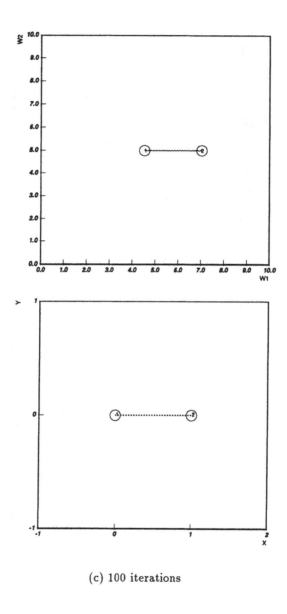

(c) 100 iterations

Figure 4.10, continued.

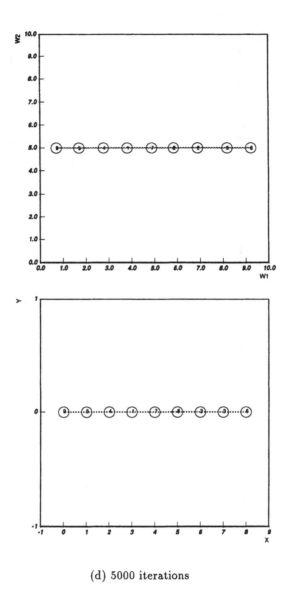

(d) 5000 iterations

Figure 4.10, continued.

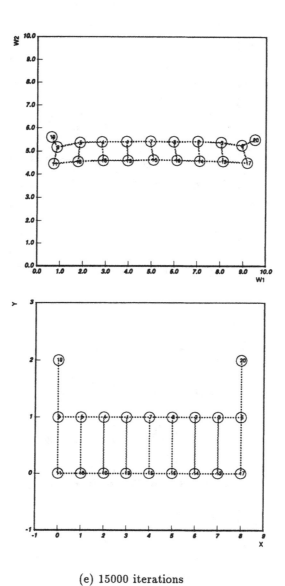

(e) 15000 iterations

Figure 4.10, continued.

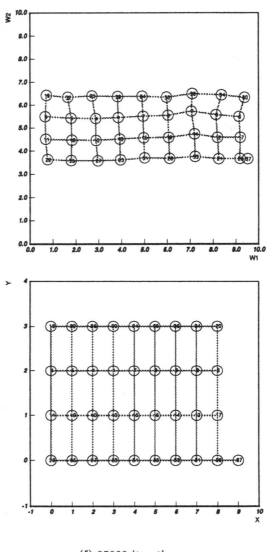

(f) 25000 iterations

Figure 4.10, continued.

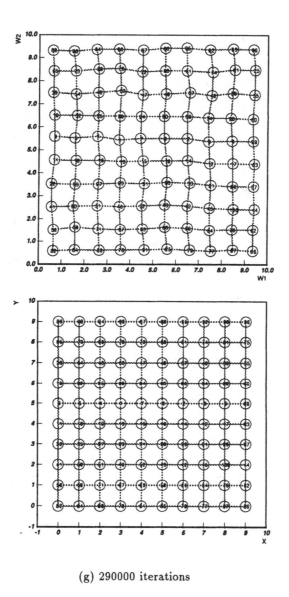

(g) 290000 iterations

Figure 4.10, continued.

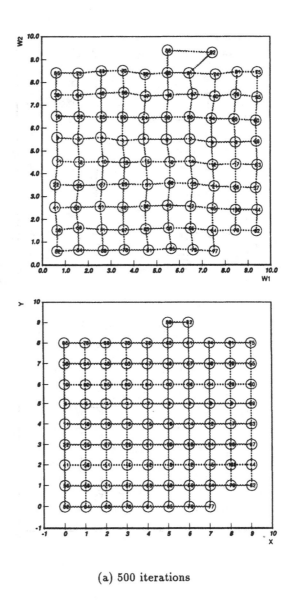

(a) 500 iterations

Figure 4.11: An example showing the network reduction process.
See the caption of Figure 4.10 for the meaning of symbols.

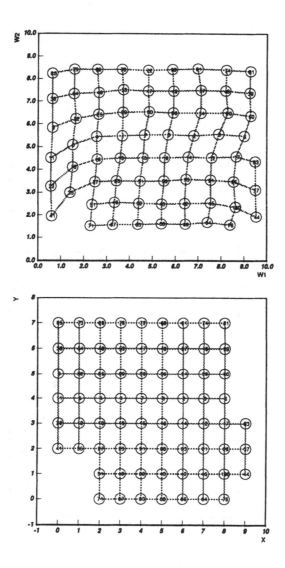

(c) 50000 iterations

Figure 4.11, continued.

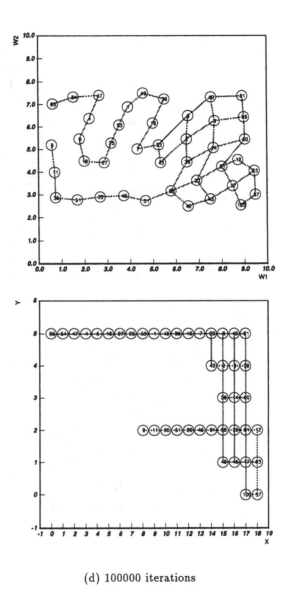

(d) 100000 iterations

Figure 4.11, continued.

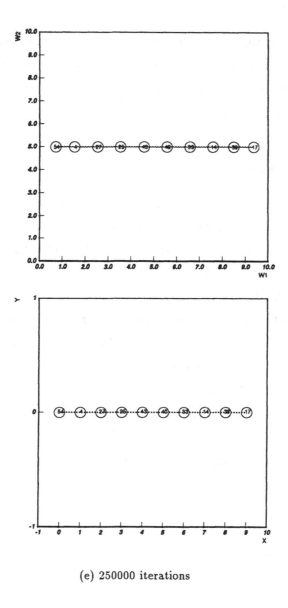

(e) 250000 iterations

Figure 4.11, continued.

we can see from the graphs, redundant neurons are killed and axes are merged; finally the lattice is reduced to a one-dimensional structure as the the source signal space becomes one dimensional. We use $\epsilon_a = 0.2$ and $\epsilon_\Theta = \frac{\pi}{6}$ for this case.

4.8 Summary

In this chapter, I have described in detail the multi-level operation of an S-Level competitive signal clustering network—SPAN. A fully parallel implementation of SPAN can display all 4 behavior features (**B.I** - **B.IV**) shown in Figure 1.2. The paradigms utilized in SPAN are **P.I**, **P.II**, **P.III**, **P.V**, **P.VI**, **P.VII.III**, and **P.VIII**.

SPAN can be considered the extension of Kohonen's SOFM to include structure level adaptation capability. The most attractive features of SPAN are that it can map the local context of the source signal space *conformally* onto a lattice structure and can adapt the lattice structure to follow the statistics of the source signals. In the next chapter, I will show an example of applying the SPAN model to an adaptive source coding system for digital communication.

Chapter 5

Application Example: An Adaptive Neural Network Source Coder

5.1 Introduction

In this chapter, I apply the S-Level network SPAN introduced in Chapter 4 to source coding problems for digital communication. The basic idea is to use SPAN as *an active codebook* that can grow from scratch to follow the statistics of source signals, capture the local context of the source signal space, and map onto the structure of the network. As a result, when the statistics of the source signals change, the network can dynamically modify its structure to follow the change.

The major advantage of using SPAN as the codebook of a vector quantizer is that SPAN can capture the local context of the source signal space. A fast codebook searching method utilizing the local context of the lattice is proposed and a novel coding scheme, called the *path*

135

coding method, is introduced to eliminate the correlation buried in the source sequence. The performance of the proposed coder is compared with an LBG coder on synthesized Gauss-Markov sources. Simulation results show that without using the path coding method, SPAN performs similarly to an LBG coder; however if the path coding method is used, SPAN performs much better than the LBG coder for highly correlated signal sources.

Finally, this chapter describes the complete system structure of a fully adaptive source coder/decoder and outlines the operational procedure for this system. Because the training method is smooth and incremental, SPAN is suitable as the basis for an adaptive vector quantization system.

5.2   Vector Quantization Problem

In recent years, much interest has been focused on *Vector Quantization (VQ)* for different physical signal sources, especially speech and image signals [46, 97, 41]. The driving forces behind this trend are listed in the following:

- According to Shannon's rate-distortion theory, a better performance is always achievable in theory by coding a block of signals (i.e. vectors) instead of coding each signal individually [122, 123, 39, 17, 132, 47, 44].

- Technology improvements, especially progress in VLSI computation ability and memory capacity, make more sophisticated coding/decoding systems possible.

- As technology enhancement advances, the requirements placed on communication sub-systems become more and more demanding.

Several key driving technologies strongly require data compression techniques; examples are high definition TV and integrated service data networks.

- The nature of the signals to be represented in computers moves from artificial signals (like symbols, texts, etc.) to signals closer to those in the physical world (e.g. sound, images, etc.), which tend to be more unpredicatable and hard to characterize analytically. Because of this, flexible and adaptable signal representation schemes will become more and more important in the near future.

Vector quantization can be viewed as a mapping Q from a k-dimensional vector space R^k into a finite subset W of R^k:

$$Q : R^k \to W, \qquad\qquad (5.1)$$

where $W = \{\mathbf{w}_i \mid i = 1, 2, \cdots, M\}$ is the set of reproduction vectors and M is the number of vectors in W. Each $\mathbf{w}_i$ in W is called a *codeword* and W is called the *codebook* for the vector quantizer. For every source vector $\mathbf{x}$, a codeword $\mathbf{w}_j$ in W is selected as the representation for $\mathbf{x}$. This process is called the *quantization phase* (or the *codebook search phase*) of the vector quantizer, denoted by $Q(\mathbf{x}) = \mathbf{w}_j$. Then the codeword $\mathbf{w}_j$ is represented by some symbols (normally the address of the codeword in the codebook) and transmitted through the channel. This process is called the *encoding phase* of the vector quantizer. On the other side of the channel, the received symbols are used to select the codewords from the codebook to reproduce the source signals. This process is called the *decoding phase* of the vector quantizer. The average number of bits required to represent the symbols in the encoding phase is the *rate* of the quantizer, and the average quantization error between input source signals and their reproduction codewords is the *distortion* of the vector quantizer. Increasing the number of codewords in the codebook can decrease the distortion of a vector quantizer, and normally will increase the rate also.

The major concern for vector quantizer design is the trade-off between distortion and rate. Linde, Buzo, and Gray [80] pointed out that the *necessary condition* for an optimum codebook is that each codeword be the centroid of the set of source signals it is representing. This suggests a *fixed point method* for generating the codebook. The idea is shown in the following algorithm:

Algorithm 5.1 (LBG Algorithm) :

1. *The codewords partition the source signal space into regions according to closest neighbor relationship.*

2. *The centroids of the partitions generate another set of codewords.*

3. *The above process continues until the codebook converges to a fixed point in the solution space of codebooks.*

◇

In most cases, the codebooks generated by this algorithm display at least a local optimum distortion rate performance if the algorithm converges during the codebook generation process [80, 44]. This algorithm is commonly referred to as the *LBG algorithm* or the *generalized Lloyd algorithm* because it is a generalized version of the scaler quantization algorithm proposed by Lloyd [81] in 1957.

A second important issue in vector quantizer design is codebook search efficiency. The major concern here is how to develop efficient ways of searching through the codebook in order to find the optimum reproduction codewords for the source signals. This is normally done by incorporating some structure into the codebook to help the search process. For example, if we incorporate a tree structure in the codebook, the search time is a logarithmic function of the size of the code book [22, 44].

5.3 VQ Using Neural Network Paradigms

There are several important problems not addressed by the LBG algorithm:

- Some codewords might be underused. In the LBG algorithm, all the codewords share the same rate (i.e. all of them are represented by the same number of bits), but not each of them contributes equally to the average system distortion; as a result, some codewords do not share the same *representation load* as others. In the extreme case, some codewords may never be accessed.

- If the statistics of the source signal change, the codebooks on both sides of the channel should be adapted to reflect the changes. The desirable adaptation should be in a smooth and incremental manner.

Several researchers have addressed the problems above by using neural network paradigms. For example, Kohonen [65] proposed a self-organization neural network vector quantizer that incorporates local interactions between codewords to form a topological feature map that *topologically sorts* the codewords on a lattice. Kohonen's vector quantizer has also been used to code images and shows similar performance to that of the LBG algorithm [98, 99, 10]. Krishnamurhty [10] proposed using an access frequency sensitive distortion measure that selects the codewords in order to avoid the codebook underuse problem.

In all the neural network coding systems mentioned above, the structures of the networks are fixed; this would greatly limit the adaptive behavior of the system. In this section, I will describe a source coding system based on SPAN. Because the structure of SPAN is adaptable, it can better capture the statistical property of the pattern space than previous source coding systems based on neural network models.

5.3.1 Basic Properties

Based on the simulation results presented in Chapter 4, we know that SPAN has the following features:

- The spatial context of the input pattern space is preserved on the local structure of the lattice; that is, the structural relationships between neurons capture the local structure of the source signal distribution.

- If the structure of the input pattern space changes with time, the network can adapt its structure to follow the change.

- The network adaptation process is incremental and is done through local interaction between neurons; hence no global structural information is required.

For most kinds of physical sources, the adjacent signals in a series tend to be highly correlated. For example, adjacent pixel blocks are similar in images and neighboring frames of LPC parameters in speech representation tend to be alike. This is because most of the physical signal generating mechanisms can only change gradually and continuously. This phenomenon can be transformed into the representation of a vector quantizer in which the adjacent source signals tend to fall into the Voronoi regions that are close in the pattern space.

The above observation suggests that we can utilize the features of SPAN in two phases of the coding process:

1. **Codebook search phase:** The local context within neuron neighborhoods can be used to guide the codebook search process.

2. **Encoding phase:** If we encode only the lattice displacement vector between neurons representing adjacent source signals; and if the coding scheme is such that the shorter lattice displacement vector requires fewer bits, then the bit rate for the whole sequence of source vectors can be minimized. Following this idea, I develop a coding scheme, called the *path coding method*, for SPAN.

The following two subsections describe the codebook searching process and the encoding method used in the SPAN source coder.

5.3.2 Fast Codebook Search Procedure

Suppose l_{old} is the lattice position of the previously selected neuron. If the current source signal is $\mathbf{x}$, then the codebook search procedure is as follows:

Algorithm 5.2 (Fast Codebook Search) :

begin

      $l_{try} \leftarrow l_{old}$

      while $(\neg(\|\mathbf{x} - \mathbf{y}(l_{try})\| \leq \|\mathbf{x} - \mathbf{y}(l_k)\|, \forall k \in \mathcal{N}(l_{try})))$

            $\Delta l \leftarrow$ the lattice index of the point in $\mathcal{L}(l_{try})$ closest to $(\mathbf{x} - \mathbf{y}(l_{try}))$

            $l_{try} \leftarrow l_{try} + \Delta l$

      end

      $l_{new} \leftarrow l_{try}$

end

$\diamond$

where $\mathbf{y}(l_{try})$ is the codeword for the neuron at lattice position l_{try}; $\mathcal{N}(l_{try})$ is the neighborhood of the neuron at l_{try}; l_k is the lattice index for neuron k; $\mathcal{L}(l_{try})$ is the lattice spaned by the local axes of neuron l_{try} [1] and l_{new} is the lattice index for the newly selected neuron (i.e , the neuron to represent $\mathbf{x}$).

Basically, the above procedure repeatedly uses local axes of neurons to find the next trial position on the lattice until the closest neighbor to the source signal is found.

If the codewords are addressed by their indices in the lattice, then the number of table accesses in the search process depends only on how accurately the difference between source signal and the previous codeword can be represented by the local lattice within the neighborhood of the previously selected neuron. For highly correlated signal sources, the search complexity tends to be of order $O(1)$ on the number of codewords in the codebook. This is better than the search complexity $O(log(n))$ for tree structured codebooks, and the complexity $O(n)$ for full search

---

[1] At any moment, each neuron can be uniquely designated by its position in the lattice, hence we may just use the lattice position to denote a neuron.

codebooks.

5.3.3 Path Coding Method

The path coding method can be considered a DPCM on the lattice or a vector version of delta modulation, where only the information about lattice displacements between adjacent selected codewords is transmitted through the channel. To represent the lattice displacement, we encode only the transition from each neuron to the neurons in its neighborhood. If a lattice displacement vector is beyond the neighborhood region, then it is represented by the concatenation of transitions. The series of transitions needed to represent a lattice displacement vector from one neuron position to the other neuron position forms a "path" between the two neurons.

The following table shows a possible coding scheme for the transitions in the 2D MHNS (minimum homogeneous neighborhood system):

Transition	code
$(0,0) \rightarrow (0,0)$	0
$(0,0) \rightarrow (1,0)$	100
$(0,0) \rightarrow (0,1)$	101
$(0,0) \rightarrow (-1,0)$	110
$(0,0) \rightarrow (0,-1)$	111

The code for a path is the concatenation of transition codes. Figure 5.1 shows an example of the path code.

To make the sequence of path codes *uniquely decodable*, we need to specify the end of each path if the path code is not 0. This can be done by adding a 0 at the end of each path. By coding in this way, a simple finite state automata can be used to uniquely decode the path sequence.

The following table lists some examples of path sequence codes; each pair of adjacent path codes in a sequence is separated by a blank in order to make the codes more understandable to the readers.

Path Sequence	Code
(0,0)(0,0)(0,0)(1,0)(0,0)	0 0 0 1000 0
(1,0)(0,-2)	1000 1111110
(0,0)(2,0)(0,1)(0,0)(0,0)	0 1001000 1010 0 0

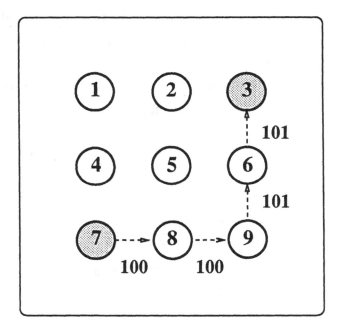

Figure 5.1: A path code example: code for the path from 7 to 3 is "100100101101".

5.3.4 Performance Comparison

I compare the performance of the SPAN coder with the LBG coder on 2D Gauss-Markov (GM) sources, which are defined by the following difference equation:

$$\mathbf{x}[n] = a\mathbf{x}[n-1] + \mathbf{g}[n], \tag{5.2}$$

where a is the autoregression constant and $\{\mathbf{g}[n]\}$ is a sequence of zero-mean, independent, identically-distributed Gaussian random variables. Here only the highly correlated case of $a = 1$ is considered. [2] The similarity between adjacent source vectors is then controlled by the variance σ^2 of $\{\mathbf{g}[n]\}$. The signal source $\mathbf{x}$ is two-dimensional and distributed within the region of $(0,0) \leq (x_1, x_2) \leq (10, 10)$, where x_1 and x_2 are the 1st and 2nd components of $\mathbf{x}$ respectively.

I simulate the operation of LBG and SPAN with the source model defined above for different σ's. Table 5.3.4 (a) and (b) summarizes the simulation results showing the coding performance for an LBG coder and a SPAN coder using the path coding method respectively. For an LBG coder, the distortion and rate are essentially insensitive to σ; hence for every codeword number, only one distortion is listed in Table 5.3.4(a). On the other hand, Table 5.3.4(b) shows that the rate decreases with σ; hence with the path coding method, the smaller the σ the better the performance of SPAN.

Figure 5.2 shows the distortion rate curves generated by the data in Table 5.3.4. Comparing the distortion rate curves for LBG and SPAN coders yields several interesting points:

- When SPAN coder does not use the path coding method (fixed rate), if performs similarly as the LBG coder.

- When SPAN coder uses the path coding method, it performs much better than the LBG coder for highly correlated sources.

---

[2]In such a case, $\{\mathbf{x}[n]\}$ is actually reduced to a Wiener process.

No. of Codewords	Rate (in bits)	Average Distortion
1	0	15.23827
2	1	9.993180
4	2	3.805799
8	3	2.169564
16	4	1.020008
32	5	0.5383006
64	6	0.2760772
128	7	0.1385902

(a) LBG coder

σ	No. of Codewords	Lattice Size	Average Path Length	Average Rate	Average Distortion
1.0	6	3×2	0.26275001	1.788233	2.852761
	9	3×3	0.3443333	2.032989	1.774432
	12	4×3	0.4365917	2.309767	1.383733
	25	5×5	0.6898200	3.069456	0.6541284
	48	8×6	1.017548	4.052642	0.3557738
	100	10×10	1.496417	5.489250	0.1655245
	132	12×11	1.731668	6.195004	0.1259496
0.5	6	3×2	0.1338500	1.401533	2.998598
	9	3×3	0.1670444	1.501122	1.809933
	12	4×3	0.2109750	1.632917	1.396291
	25	5×5	0.3325640	1.997688	0.6550556
	48	8×6	0.5022479	2.506742	0.3548502
	100	10×10	0.7475840	3.242751	0.1648479
	132	12×11	0.8727659	3.618297	0.1256384
0.2	6	3×2	5.61×10^{-2}	1.168283	3.014576
	9	3×3	6.227778×10^{-2}	1.186822	1.874519
	12	4×3	8.1325×10^{-2}	1.243967	1.449642
	25	5×5	1.3254×10^{-1}	1.397616	0.6743547
	48	8×6	1.982792×10^{-1}	1.594835	0.3606514
	100	10×10	2.94362×10^{-1}	1.883085	0.1653093
	132	12×11	3.422167×10^{-1}	2.026649	0.1259553

(b) SPAN coder with path coding method

Table 5.1: The performance of SPAN and LBG coders on Gauss-Markov Sources; the source signals are distributed uniformly in the region $(0,0) \leq (x_1, x_2) \leq (10,10)$, σ is the standard deviation of the Gaussian component in the Gauss-Markov source; the average path length is the average number of neighborhood transitions required to specify the displacement vector between adjacent source vectors in the training sequence.

- The higher the degree of similarity between adjacent source vectors, the better the performance of SPAN is by using the path coding method.

- As σ decreases, the rate becomes less sensitive to the size of the codebook. This means that the rate *does not scale up* with the codebook when the signal source is highly correlated.

In general, by using the path coding method, the bit rate is dependent on the correlation between source signals and is quite insensitive to the size of the codebook. Great benefits can be gained by using this method when source signals are highly correlated.

However, if the source signals are totally uncorrelated, the path coding method might perform worse than the LBG algorithm. When this situation occurs, the system should switch back to the normal encoding scheme while still using a SPAN codebook; in this way, performance as good as the LBG coder can be retained. This "switching process" should not be too difficult to implement; we must only periodically check the *average path length* between adjacent selected codewords in SPAN coder. If the average path is too long, then switch back to the normal coding scheme. Of course, the same decision criteria should be used on both sides of the channel.

Figure 5.3 shows the codebook searching performance using our proposed fast codebook search procedure. Notice that the codebook searching time is quite insensitive to the size of the codebook.

5.3.5 Adaptive SPAN Coder/Decoder

Since the adaptation process of SPAN is incremental and requires only local operation on the lattice, we can use this property to design an

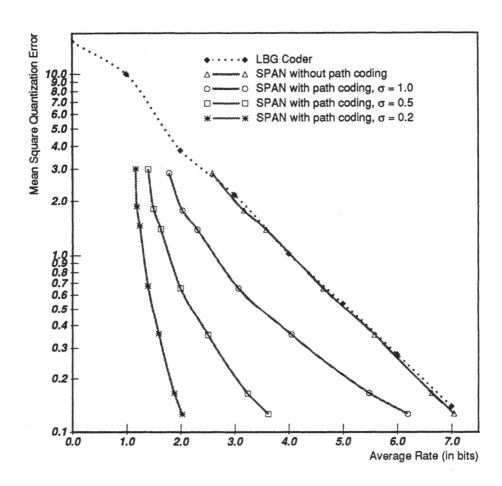

Figure 5.2: Performance comparison between LBG and SPAN coder on Gauss-Markov sources.

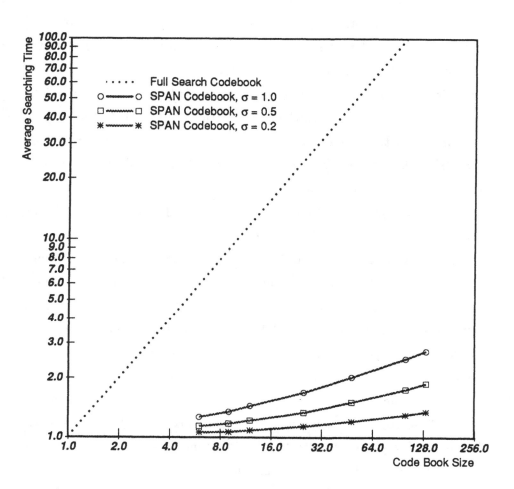

Figure 5.3: Codebook searching efficiency of SPAN coder using fast codebook search procedure.

adaptive vector quantizer. Figure 5.4 shows a proposed adaptive source coding system based on the SPAN codebook.

As shown in Figure 5.4, at time index n, the input source vector $\mathbf{x}[n]$ is fed into the coder. The neuron in SPAN with input weight vector closest to $\mathbf{x}[n]$ is then selected. If we let $\mathbf{l}[n]$ be the lattice position of the selected neuron and $\mathbf{y}(\mathbf{l}[n])$ be the codeword (i.e. the input weight vector) for neuron $\mathbf{l}[n]$, $\mathbf{d}[n]$, the lattice path from $\mathbf{l}[n-1]$ to $\mathbf{l}[n]$, is then encoded using the path coding method to generate path code $c[n]$, where $\mathbf{l}[n-1]$ is the lattice position of the previously selected neuron. $c[n]$ is then sent through the *main channel*.

To enable the adaptation process on both sides of the channel, the residue vector $\mathbf{e}[n] = \mathbf{x}[n] - \mathbf{y}(\mathbf{l}[n])$ is encoded and the code $r[n]$ representing the residue codeword $\hat{\mathbf{e}}[n]$ is sent through the *side channel*. The residue codeword $\hat{\mathbf{e}}[n]$ is then used to activate the network adaptation process of SPAN on both sides of the channel (equivalently, on both sides of the channel, the SPAN codebooks see the same input signal $\hat{\mathbf{x}}[n] = \mathbf{y}(\mathbf{l}[n]) + \hat{\mathbf{e}}[n]$, and hence will adapt themselves with the same pace).

The residue encoding is carried out by a small size *lattice quantizer* in which no codebook is needed. [3] We can encode the lattice positions in the residue space using the path coding method (i.e., we encode the difference between lattice positions and the origin).

Initially, we can have codebooks with the same initial random condition on both sides of the channel (for instance, when both have one

---

[3]In lattice quantizer, the space of interests is decomposed regularly by a lattice structure [25]. Every codeword in the quantizer is a lattice point in the source signal space. Since lattice points in the source signal space can be derived through some simple calculation, no codebook storage is necessary. [26] has developed a series of coding/decoding algorithms for lattice quantizers.

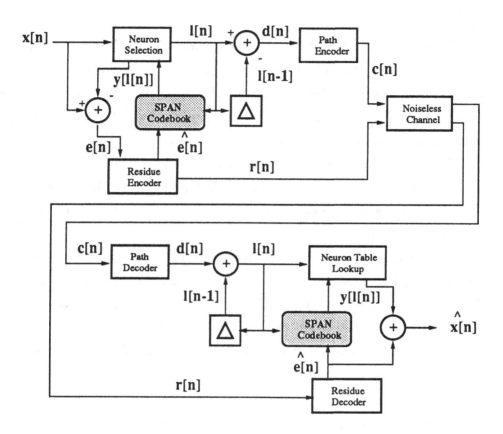

Figure 5.4: A proposed adaptive SPAN coding/decoding system. $\mathbf{x}[n]$ is the source vector at time n; $\mathbf{l}[n]$ is the lattice position of the neuron with input weight vector closest to $\mathbf{x}[n]$; $\mathbf{y}(\mathbf{l}[n])$ is the input weight vector for the neuron located at $\mathbf{l}[n]$ in the lattice; $\mathbf{d}[n]$ is the lattice displacement vector from the lattice position of the previously selected neuron to that of the current neuron; $\mathbf{c}[n]$ is the path code for $\mathbf{d}[n]$; $\mathbf{e}[n]$ is the vector difference between $\mathbf{x}[n]$ and $\mathbf{y}(\mathbf{l}[n])$; $\hat{\mathbf{e}}[n]$ is the quantized version of $\mathbf{e}[n]$ through the residue encoder; $\mathbf{r}[n]$ is the code for $\hat{\mathbf{e}}[n]$; and $\hat{\mathbf{x}}[n]$ is the signal regenerated at the receiver end.

neuron residing at the origin). Then as the source signals come in, the codebooks will evolve with the same pace in order to follow the signal statistics on both sides of the channel. In the beginning, most of the information is sent through the side channel; then gradually as the structure of the codebooks is built up and approaches that of the source signal space, more and more information is sent through the main channel. Eventually, as most of the information is transmitted through the main channel, the side channel is *shut off*. Later on, if the statistics of the source signal change, the side channel will *wake up* and the adaptation cycle will start again.

Better performance can be obtained by further incorporating some predictive coding mechanism into the encoding part of the system. The function of the predictive mechanism is to predict the next codeword position in the lattice based on previously selected neuron positions. The difference in lattice position between the actually selected codeword and the predicted codeword is encoded using the path coding method.

5.4   Summary

The coding/decoding system presented in this chapter can be viewed as an attempt to cover two major trends in vector quantizer design. The first trend is to generate internal structure for the codebook. As the signal sources become more and more complicated, there is a growing effort to develop codebooks with an internal structure that reflects some aspect of the signal space in order to enhance the codeword search process [21, 22]. The other trend is to incorporate feedback and internal states into the encoder to eliminate the correlation between source signals in the sequence [20, 30, 37]. In this case, the codes are sensitive to the context of the source sequence and finite state automata models are used to capture the local context buried in the sequence, so as to eliminate correlations.

In this chapter, I have shown that by utilizing the local context built in the lattice, we can achieve both fast codebook searching (to enhance encoding efficiency) and source signal correlation elimination (to enhance distortion rate performance) under our proposed framework.

Future work can be done in trying the SPAN coder/decoder scheme on physical sources such as image, speech, etc. It is also possible to apply this model to multi-media coding systems to allocate bits among several channels. In this case, each channel is taken care of by a SPAN; in addition an arbitration mechanism can be added on top of the group of SPANs to adjust the threshold parameters (e.g. ϵ_d, ϵ_a, etc.) of the networks; thus would optimize the global system performance.

Chapter 6

Conclusions

6.1 Contributions

The *contribution tree* shown in Figure 1.3 outlines the contributions of this monograph. To be more specific, this study has achieved the following:

1. Set up a formal conceptual structure (ontology) for multi-level adaptation of discrete time artificial neural network systems .

2. Developed methods to decide the minimum delay for signal propagation through the network thus ensuring state consistency.

3. Introduced an *activity-based structure level adaptation paradigm* as a general guideline for the structure level adaptation of neural network systems. In particular, I proposed a general procedure for designing adaptable structure neural networks and listed the criteria for guiding the firing of various structural operators.

4. Defined an adaptable structure multi-layer feed-forward neural network, *FUNNET (FUNction NETwork)* under the general S-Net

formalism defined in the multi-level adaptation ontology.

5. Defined the *Fluctuated Distortion Measure* for guiding the neuron generation process for FUNNET.

6. Proposed a representation scheme for FUNNET using doubly linked lists. This network representation scheme can support all the required structure level operations, such as changing the number of layers, generating/annihilating the neurons within each layers, and modifying the interconnections between neurons in adjacent layers.

7. Implemented a software simulation tool for FUNNET based on the proposed representation scheme.

8. Defined a competitive signal clustering network, *SPAN (Space PArtition Network)*, which takes Kohonen's *SOFM (Self-Organization Feature Map)* as a P-Level special case; developed structure level adaptation algorithms for SPAN.

9. Formulated the parameter level adaptation convergence theory for SPAN under a distributed energy function formalism (i.e., each neuron has its own local energy function), and proved that the asymptotic weight vector for each neuron minimizes its own energy function.

10. Proposed a representation scheme for SPAN that encodes a variable dimension, adjustable size lattice structure which can support all the structural operators required by the *SEA (Structure Evolution Automata)* of SPAN.

11. Implemented a software simulator for SPAN based on the proposed representation scheme.

12. Developed an adaptive vector quantization source coding system based on SPAN.

13. Proposed methods for enhancing rate-distortion performance (the path coding method), fast encoding/decoding (fast codebook search method), and dynamically adjusting the structure of the codebook (codebook adaptation).

6.2 Recommendations

Future research directions can follow the possible paths for growing the contribution tree. In particular, Figure 6.1 displays some immediate descendants of the current entities that are worth exploring (in shaded boxes surrounded by dashed lines):

- Applying the multi-level adaptation formalism for modeling, analyzing, designing and implementing discrete time artificial neural network systems.

- Applying the activity-based structure-level adaptation paradigm to other current parameter level neural network models to develop the corresponding S-Nets.

- Applying FUNNET to function mapping and classification problems in various domains and comparing the results with currently fixed structure multi-layer feed-forward networks.

- Exploring the possibility of designing special purpose hardware for FUNNET based on the proposed representation scheme.

- Applying SPAN to other applications like pattern recognition, sequence classification, or dimension reduction problems.

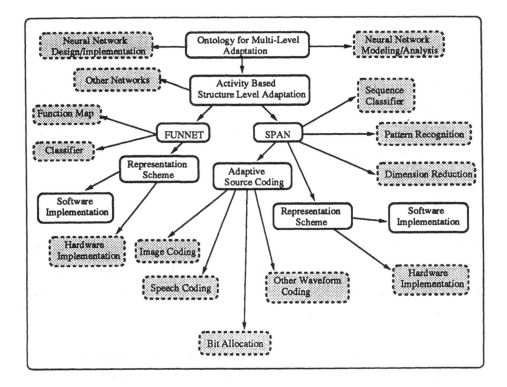

Figure 6.1: Future research directions.

- Designing special purpose hardware for SPAN based on the proposed flexible representation scheme for lattice structures.

- Applying the concepts developed in the adaptive source coding system to image coding, speech coding, and othe waveform coding problems.

- Applying the adaptive vector quantization technique to the bit allocation problems in multi-channel (or multi-media) transmission or storage systems.

Appendix A

Mathematical Background for Function Networks

In this Appendix, I will list and comment on the theorems relevant to the multi-level feed-forward function mapping network discussed in Chapter 3. Because the proofs can be found in other literatures [69, 83, 28], I will not supply them here.

A.1   Kolmogorov's Theorem

Theorem A.1 (Kolmogorov, 1957) :

There exist fixed continuous monotonical increasing functions $h_{pq}(x)$ *on* $\mathbf{I} = [0,1]$ *such that each continuous function for* $\mathbf{I}^m$ *can be written in the form:*

$$f(x_1,\ldots,x_m) = \sum_{q=1}^{2m+1} g_q(\sum_{p=1}^{m} h_{pq}(x_p)) \qquad (A.1)$$

where g_q *are properly chosen continuous functions of one variable.*

Basically, Kolmogorov's Theorem states that it is sufficient to "exactly" represent any multi-dimensional function by combination of single variable continuous functions and addition. This very powerful theorem suggests that functions with two variables, and functions with two variables other than addition are totally redundant. Equation(A.1) can be considered the output of a simple network with two hidden layers: the functions h_{pq} are the outputs of the first layer while the functions g_q are implemented in the second layer. In Kolmogorov's Theorem, the functions h_{pq} are specially defined and fixed independently of f while the functions g_q are determined by the particular function f.

A.2 Networks with One Hidden Layer are Sufficient

Definition A.1 (Sigmoidal Function) :
We say σ is sigmoidal *if*

$$\sigma(x) \rightarrow \begin{cases} 1 & as\ t \rightarrow +\infty \\ 0 & as\ t \rightarrow -\infty \end{cases}$$

$\diamondsuit$

In the following theorems, I use $\mathbf{I}^m$ to denote the m-dimensional unit cube, $[0,1]^m$ and use $C(\mathbf{I}^m)$ to represent the space of continuous functions on $\mathbf{I}^m$.

Theorem A.2 (Cybento, 1989) :
Let σ be any bounded, measurable sigmoidal function. Then the finite sums of the form

$$G(X) = \sum_{j=1}^{N} w_j^{(1,2)} \sigma((W_j^{(0,1)})^T X - \Theta_j)$$

are dense in $C(\mathbf{I}^m)$. In other words, given any $f \in C(\mathbf{I}^m)$ and $\epsilon > 0$, there is a sum, $G(X)$ of the above form, for which

$$|G(X) - f(X)| < \epsilon, for\ all\ X \in \mathbf{I}^m.$$

Theorem A.2 suggests that function networks with one hidden layer of neurons are sufficient to represent any $\mathcal{R}^m \to \mathcal{R}$ mapping to any desirable degree of accuracy. This theorem gives a solid theoretical groundwork for the representation power of multi-layer feed-forward neural networks.

A specialization of Theorem A.2 gives the following theorem for neural networks used as classifiers:

Theorem A.3 (Cybento, 1989) :

Let σ be a continuous sigmoidal function. Let f be the decision function for any finite measurable partition of $\mathbf{I}^m$. For any $\epsilon > 0$, there is a finite sum of the form

$$G(X) = \sum_{j=1}^{N} w_j^{(1,2)} \sigma((W_j^{(0,1)})^T X - \Theta_j)$$

and a set $D \subset \mathbf{I}^m$, such that $m(D) \geq 1 - \epsilon$ and

$$|G(X) - F(X)| < \epsilon \text{ for } X \in D$$

where $m(D)$ denotes the measure for the set D.   ◇

Appendix B

Fluctuated Distortion Measure

B.1 Measure Construction

Construction B.1 (Fluctuated Distortion Measure) :
In a multi-layer feed-forward neural network, the distortion measure

$$FD_i^{(l)} \triangleq |\delta_i^{(l)}| \, \|Q^{(l-1)}\| \, WD_i^{(l)}$$

can be used as the operation measure for the contribution of the fluctuation of the input weight vector of the ith neuron in layer l (measured by $WD_i^{(l)}$) to the total system distortion.

First we take the derivative of the overall system error with respect to the walking distance of the ith neuron in layer l:

$$
\begin{aligned}
\frac{\partial \mathcal{E}}{\partial WD_i^{(l)}} &= \left| \frac{\partial \mathcal{E}}{\partial WD_i^{(l)}} \right| = \left| \frac{\partial < \|\hat{Y} - Y\|^2 >}{\partial p_i^{(l)}} \frac{\partial p_i^{(l)}}{\partial WD_i^{(l)}} \right| \\
&= < \left| \frac{\partial \|\hat{Y} - Y\|^2}{\partial p_i^{(l)}} \right| \left| \frac{\partial p_i^{(l)}}{\partial WD_i^{(l)}} \right| > \\
&= < |\delta_i^{(l)}| \left| \frac{\partial p_i^{(l)}}{\partial WD_i^{(l)}} \right| >,
\end{aligned}
\tag{B.1}
$$

where

$$
\delta_i^{(l)} \triangleq \sigma^{(1)}(p_i^{(l)}) e_i^{(l)}
\tag{B.2}
$$

is the pre-sigmoid error propagated to the ith neuron in layer l; $e_i^{(l)}$ is the corresponding *post-sigmoid error*; $p_i^{(l)}$ is the *pre-sigmoid activity*, or *net input* for this neuron; Y is the system output vector, and $\hat{Y}$ is the desirable output vector.

Notice that the net input $p_i^{(l)}$ in (B.1) can be written as

$$
\begin{aligned}
p_i^{(l)} &= \sum_{j=0}^{K_{l-1}} q_j^{(l-1)} w_{ij}^{(l-1,l)} \\
&= (Q^{(l-1)})^T W_i^{(l-1,l)}.
\end{aligned}
\tag{B.3}
$$

Let $\Delta W_i^{(l-1,l)}$ be the fluctuation of the input weight vector $W_i^{(l-1,l)}$ around its optimal value $\widehat{W}_i^{(l-1,l)}$, i.e.

$$
W_i^{(l-1,l)} = \widehat{W}_i^{(l-1,l)} + \Delta W_i^{(l-1,l)}
$$

$\Delta W_i^{(l-1,l)}$ can be modeled as:

$$
\Delta W_i^{(l-1,l)} = WD_i^{(l-1,l)} \widehat{\omega}^{K_{l-1}}
\tag{B.4}
$$

where $\widehat{\omega}^{K_{l-1}}$ is some normalized K_{l-1} dimensional random variable. [1]
Hence, we have

$$
\begin{aligned}
\frac{\partial p_i^{(l)}}{\partial W D_i^{(l)}} &= \frac{\partial((Q^{(l-1)})^T W_i^{(l-1,l)})}{\partial W D_i^{(l)}} \\
&= (Q^{(l-1)})^T \frac{\partial W_i^{(l-1,l)}}{\partial W D_i^{(l)}} \\
&= (Q^{(l-1)})^T \widehat{\omega}^{K_{l-1}}.
\end{aligned}
\tag{B.5}
$$

Substituting (B.5) into (B.1), we have

$$
\begin{aligned}
\frac{\partial \mathcal{E}}{\partial W D_i^{(l)}} &= \;<|\delta_i^{(l)}|\,|(Q^{(l-1)})^T\,\widehat{\omega}^{K_{l-1}}|> \\
&\propto \;<|\delta_i^{(l)}|\,\|Q^{(l-1)}\|>.
\end{aligned}
\tag{B.6}
$$

Let $\Delta \mathcal{E}_i^{(l)}$ be the contribution from the WD of the ith neuron in layer l to the total system output error; we now have

$$
\begin{aligned}
\Delta \mathcal{E}_i^{(l)} &= \frac{\partial \mathcal{E}}{\partial W D_i^{(l)}} W D_i^{(l)} \\
&\propto \;<|\delta_i^{(l)}|\,\|Q^{(l-1)}\|> W D_i^{(l)} \\
&= \;<|\delta_i^{(l)}|\,\|Q^{(l-1)}\|\,W D_i^{(l)}>.
\end{aligned}
\tag{B.7}
$$

We define a distortion measure $FD_i^{(l)}$ as

$$
FD_i^{(l)} \triangleq |\delta_i^{(l)}|\,\|Q^{(l-1)}\|\,W D_i^{(l)}.
\tag{B.8}
$$

---

[1]Since WD measures the average length of the movement, it can be considered the scaling factor for the multi-dimensional random process $\Delta W_i^{(l-1,l)}$.

Now the total system distortion $\Delta \mathcal{E}_W$ owing to the fluctuation of weights can be suitably measured as follows:

$$\Delta \mathcal{E}_W = \sum_{\substack{\text{every neuron } i \text{ in every layer } l}} \Delta \mathcal{E}_i^{(l)}$$
$$\propto \sum_{\substack{\text{every neuron } i \text{ in every layer } l}} FD_i^{(l)}. \qquad (\text{B.9})$$

Hence the $FD_i^{(l)}$ defined in (B.8) can be used as the measure of the contribution of the walking distance of the ith neuron in layer l to the total system distortion. $FD_i^{(l)}$ is called the *Fluctuated Distortion Measure* for the ith neuron in layer l. $\diamond$

B.2   The Relation Between Fluctuation and Error

The fluctuated distortion is very closely related to the contribution of the input weight vector fluctuation of a neuron to the overall system output fluctuations as depicted in the following theorem:

Theorem B.1 :

In a multi-layer feed-forward network, around the vicinity of a local optimal set of weights, we have

$$\frac{\partial \mathcal{E}}{\partial W D_i^{(l)}} = \frac{\partial < \|\hat{Y} - Y\|^2 >}{\partial W D_i^{(l)}}$$

$$= \frac{\partial < \|Y - <Y>\|^2 >}{\partial W D_i^{(l)}}, \qquad \text{(B.10)}$$

where $\mathcal{E} = < \|\hat{Y} - Y\|^2 >$ is the mean square error; $\hat{Y}$ is the desirable output; and $< Y >$ is the mean value of Y.

Let $\tilde{Y}$ be the output vector generated by the optimal set of weights. Let $\mathcal{E}_{min} = < |\hat{Y} - \tilde{Y}\|^2 >$ be the minimum mean square error corresponding to the optimal weights. Let ΔY be the fluctuation of the output vector around the optimal output vector $\hat{Y}$. We have $Y = \tilde{Y} + \Delta Y$, and $\mathcal{E}$ can be written as

$$
\begin{aligned}
\mathcal{E} &= < (\hat{Y} - Y)^T (\hat{Y} - Y) > \\
&= < (\hat{Y} - \tilde{Y} - \Delta Y)^T (\hat{Y} - \tilde{Y} - \Delta Y) > \\
&= < \|\hat{Y} - \tilde{Y}\|^2 > + < \|\Delta Y\|^2 > -2 < \Delta Y^T (\hat{Y} - \tilde{Y}) > \text{(B.11)}
\end{aligned}
$$

If ΔY is a random fluctuation around the optimal output vector, then ΔY and $(\hat{Y} - \tilde{Y})$ are independent; hence

$$< \Delta Y^T (\hat{Y} - \tilde{Y}) > = < \Delta Y^T > < \hat{Y} - \tilde{Y} > \approx 0, \qquad \text{(B.12)}$$

since $< \Delta Y > \approx 0$.

Now (B.11) becomes

$$\mathcal{E} = <\|\hat{Y} - \tilde{Y}\|^2> + <\|\Delta Y\|^2>$$
$$= \mathcal{E}_{min} + <\|\Delta Y\|^2>. \tag{B.13}$$

Hence we have

$$\frac{\partial \mathcal{E}}{\partial WD_i^{(l)}} = \frac{\partial \mathcal{E}_{min}}{\partial WD_i^{(l)}} + \frac{\partial <\|\Delta Y\|^2>}{\partial WD_i^{(l)}}$$
$$= \frac{\partial <\|\Delta Y\|^2>}{\partial WD_i^{(l)}}. \tag{B.14}$$

We can now do similar manipulations with $<\|Y - <Y>\|^2>$. Since

$$Y - <Y> = \tilde{Y} + \Delta Y - <Y>, \tag{B.15}$$

we have

$$<\|Y - <Y>\|^2> = <\|\tilde{Y} - <Y>\|^2> + <\|\Delta Y\|^2>$$
$$+ 2<\Delta Y^T(\tilde{Y} - <Y>)>$$
$$= <\|\tilde{Y} - <Y>\|^2> + <\|\Delta Y\|^2>$$
$$+ 2<\Delta Y^T><\tilde{Y} - <Y>>$$
$$= <\|\tilde{Y} - <Y>\|^2> + <\|\Delta Y\|^2> \tag{B.16}$$

Now consider the following:

$$\frac{\partial <\|\tilde{Y} - <Y>\|^2>}{\partial WD_i^{(l)}} = <\frac{\partial(\|\tilde{Y} - <Y>\|^2)}{\partial WD_i^{(l)}}> \approx 0; \tag{B.17}$$

since both $\tilde{Y}$ and $<Y>$ are insensitive to the variation of $WD_i^{(l)}$.

Now taking the derivative of (B.16), we have

$$\frac{\partial < \|Y - <Y>\|^2 >}{\partial W D_i^{(l)}} = \frac{\partial < \|\Delta Y\|^2 >}{\partial W D_i^{(l)}}. \qquad (B.18)$$

From (B.14) and (B.18), we have

$$\frac{\partial \mathcal{E}}{\partial W D_i^{(l)}} = \frac{\partial < \|Y - <Y>\|^2 >}{\partial W D_i^{(l)}},$$

thus the proof.   ◇

Appendix C

SPAN Convergence Theory

In this chapter, I supply the proof for the parameter lever convergence theorem for SPAN. The first section contains the proof, and the second section defines the energy function for SPAN and relates the weight convergent property to the gradient descent algorithm.

C.1   Asymptotic Value of $\mathbf{w}_i$

Theorem C.1 :

In the SPAN model, let $y_i(\mathbf{x}) = \phi(\|\mathbf{l}_i - C(\mathbf{x})\|)$, where $\mathbf{l}_i$ is the lattice position for neuron i and $C(\mathbf{x}) = \mathbf{l}_j$ is the lattice position for neuron j that has the input weight vector closest to the input signal $\mathbf{x}$. For the sufficiently small learning rate α, the asymptotical value of the weight vector for neuron i is

$$\hat{\mathbf{w}}_i = \lim_{n \to \infty} \mathbf{w}_i[n] = \frac{\int_{\Omega_i} p(\mathbf{x}) y_i(\mathbf{x}) \mathbf{x} dx}{\int_{\Omega_i} p(\mathbf{x}) y_i(\mathbf{x}) dx},$$

where $p(\mathbf{x})$ is the probability density function for input patterns.

According to Kohonen's learning algorithm, the iteration equation for the weight adjustment of neuron i is

$$
\begin{aligned}
\mathbf{w}_i[n+1] &= \mathbf{w}_i[n] + \alpha y_i(\mathbf{x}[n+1])(\mathbf{x}[n+1] - \mathbf{w}_i[n]) \\
&= (1 - \alpha y_i(\mathbf{x}[n+1]))\mathbf{w}_i[n] + \alpha y_i(\mathbf{x}[n+1])\mathbf{x}[n+1] \\
&= (1 - \alpha y_i(\mathbf{x}[n+1]))((1 - \alpha y_i(\mathbf{x}[n]))\mathbf{w}_i[n-1] \\
&\quad + \alpha y_i(\mathbf{x}[n])\mathbf{x}[n]) + \alpha y_i(\mathbf{x}[n+1])\mathbf{x}[n+1] \\
&= (\prod_{k=0}^{n}(1 - \alpha y_i(\mathbf{x}[n+1-k])))\mathbf{w}_i[0] \\
&\quad + \alpha \sum_{j=1}^{n+1}(y_i(\mathbf{x}[j]) \prod_{k=j+1}^{n+1}{}^{+}(1 - \alpha y_i(\mathbf{x}[k])))\mathbf{x}[j], \qquad (\text{C.1})
\end{aligned}
$$

where

$$\prod_{k=i}^{j}{}^{+} = \begin{cases} \prod_{k=i}^{j} & \text{if } j \geq i \\ 1 & \text{otherwise.} \end{cases} \tag{C.2}$$

In equation(C.1),

$$\lim_{n\to\infty} (\prod_{k=0}^{n}(1 - \alpha y_i(\mathbf{x}[n+1-k]))) = 0; \tag{C.3}$$

hence

$$\widehat{\mathbf{w}}_i \triangleq \lim_{n\to\infty} \mathbf{w}_i[n]$$

$$= \lim_{n\to\infty} \alpha \sum_{j=1}^{n}(y_i(\mathbf{x}[j])\mathbf{x}[j] \prod_{k=j+1}^{n}{}^{+}(1 - \alpha y_i(\mathbf{x}[k]))). \tag{C.4}$$

We know that $y_i(\mathbf{x}) \neq 0$ iff $\mathbf{x} \in V_j$ for some $j \in \mathcal{N}_i$, where V_j is the Voronoi region for neuron j and $\mathcal{N}_i$ is the neighborhood set of neuron i. Let $y_i(\mathbf{x}) = Y_{ij}$ when $\mathbf{x} \in V_j$ and let

$$\gamma_i(m) \triangleq \prod_{k=n-m+1}^{n}(1 - \alpha y_i(\mathbf{x}[k])) = \prod_{j}(1 - \alpha Y_{ij})^{m_j}, \tag{C.5}$$

where m_j is the the number of occurrence of $\mathbf{x}$ in V_j during the period of m samples.

For α sufficiently small, $\gamma_i(m)$ can be approximated by

$$\gamma_i(m) \simeq \prod_{j}(1 - m_j\alpha Y_{ij}) \simeq 1 - \alpha \sum_{j} m_j Y_{ij}. \tag{C.6}$$

We know also $\sum_j m_j = m$ and $P(j) \simeq \frac{m_j}{m}$ as m becomes large, where $P(j)$ is the probability mass function of the occurrence of the input signal in V_j, i.e. $P(j) = \int_{V_j} p(\mathbf{x})d\mathbf{x}$. Hence for large m, following equation(C.6), we have

$$\gamma_i(m) \simeq 1 - m\alpha \sum_j P(j)Y_{ij} = 1 - \alpha m\chi_i \triangleq \hat{\gamma}_i(m), \qquad (C.7)$$

where $\chi_i \triangleq \sum_j P(j)Y_{ij}$.

If α is sufficiently small, then we have $\gamma_i(m) \simeq 1$. Assume $\mathbf{x}[n]$ is a stationary process; then $y_i(\mathbf{x}[n])$ is also stationary. For large m, we have

$$\prod_{k=n-m+1}^{n} (1 - \alpha y_i(\mathbf{x}[k])) \simeq \prod_{k=n-2m+1}^{n-m} (1 - \alpha y_i(\mathbf{x}[k]))$$

$$\simeq \prod_{k=n-(j+1)m+1}^{n-jm} (1 - \alpha y_i(\mathbf{x}[k]))$$

$$\simeq \hat{\gamma}_i(m), \ 0 \le j \le \frac{n}{m} - 1. \qquad (C.8)$$

Using the approximations above, if we partition the summation in equation(C.4) into n/m smaller summations with m terms in each summation, we have

$$\hat{\mathbf{w}}_i \simeq \lim_{n \to \infty} \alpha\Big(\sum_{j=n-m+1}^{n} y_i(\mathbf{x}[j])\mathbf{x}[j] + \hat{\gamma}_i(m) \sum_{j=n-2m+1}^{n-m} y_i(\mathbf{x}[j])\mathbf{x}[j] + \cdots$$

$$+ (\hat{\gamma}_i(m))^{n/m-1} \sum_{j=1}^{m} y_i(\mathbf{x}[j])\mathbf{x}[j]\Big). \qquad (C.9)$$

Let

$$\bar{q}_i = E(y_i(\mathbf{x})\mathbf{x}) = \sum_k P(k)Y_{ik}E(\mathbf{x} \mid \mathbf{x} \in V_k) = \sum_k P(k)Y_{ik}\mathbf{X}_k, \qquad (C.10)$$

where $\mathbf{X}_k$ is the centroid of Voronoid region V_k.

Then equation(C.9) can be simplified to

$$
\begin{aligned}
\widehat{\mathbf{w}}_i &\simeq \alpha \lim_{n\to\infty} (m\bar{q}_i \sum_{k=0}^{n/m-1} \gamma_i(m)^k) \simeq \frac{\alpha m \bar{q}_i}{1 - \gamma_i(m)} = \frac{\alpha m \bar{q}_i}{\alpha m \chi_i} = \frac{\bar{q}_i}{\chi_i} \\
&= \frac{\sum_k P(k) Y_{ik} X_k}{\sum_k P(k) Y_{ik}} = \frac{\int_V p(\mathbf{x}) y_i(\mathbf{x}) \mathbf{x} d\mathbf{x}}{\int_V p(\mathbf{x}) y_i(\mathbf{x}) d\mathbf{x}} \\
&= \frac{\int_{\Omega_i} p(\mathbf{x}) y_i(\mathbf{x}) \mathbf{x} d\mathbf{x}}{\int_{\Omega_i} p(\mathbf{x}) y_i(\mathbf{x}) d\mathbf{x}} .
\end{aligned} \tag{C.11}
$$

Notice that in the volumn integration above, we replaced the integration range of V by Ω_i. The reason we can do that is because $y_i(\mathbf{x})$ is non-zero only in Ω_i. Thus the proof. $\diamond$

C.2 Energy Function and Gradient Descent

Definition C.1 (Energy Function) :

The energy function for neuron i in SPAN can be defined as

$$
\varepsilon_i \triangleq \frac{1}{2} E\{y_i \|\mathbf{x} - \mathbf{w}_i\|^2\}, \tag{C.12}
$$

where y_i is the output level for neuron i; $\mathbf{x}$ is the input vector to the network; and $\mathbf{w}_i$ is the input weight vector of neuron i. $\diamond$

With the energy function defined in Definition C.1, we can show that the parameter adaptation process defined in Chapter 4 performs gradient descent in the energy surface of each individual neuron. Using the gradient descent algorithm, we have

$$
\Delta \mathbf{w}_i = -\alpha \nabla_{w_i} \varepsilon_i
$$

$$\begin{aligned}
&= -\frac{1}{2}\alpha E\{\nabla_{w_i}(y_i\|\mathbf{x} - \mathbf{w}_i\|^2)\} \\
&\approx -\frac{1}{2}\alpha E\{y_i \nabla_{w_i}(\|\mathbf{x} - \mathbf{w}_i\|^2)\} \\
&= -\frac{1}{2}\alpha E\{y_i(-2(\mathbf{x} - \mathbf{w}_i))\} \\
&= \alpha E\{y_i(\mathbf{x} - \mathbf{w}_i)\}.
\end{aligned} \qquad (C.13)$$

The term inside the E in (C.13), $y_i(\mathbf{x} - \mathbf{w}_i)$, is exactly the formula used in the parameter adaptation process of SPAN, except in SPAN, $y_i[n]$ is approximated by $\phi[n](\|\mathbf{l}_i - \mathbf{l}_k\|)$, where $\mathbf{l}_k$ is the lattice position of the neuron with the highest output activity at time index n.

With the energy function for the neurons defined in Definition C.1, the following theorem states that the asymptotic value of the weight vector of each neuron optimizes its energy function.

Theorem C.2 (Asymptotic Weight Vector is Optimal) :
The asymptotic weight vector $\widehat{\mathbf{w}}_i$ for neuron i,

$$\widehat{\mathbf{w}}_i[n] = \frac{\int_{\Omega_i} p(\mathbf{x})y_i(\mathbf{x})\mathbf{x}\,dx}{\int_{\Omega_i} p(\mathbf{x})y_i(\mathbf{x})\,dx},$$

minimizes the energy function ε_i for neuron i.

If the optimal weight vector $\widehat{\mathbf{w}}_i$ is reached, we have

$$\nabla_{w_i} \varepsilon_i \mid_{\widehat{w}_i} = 0. \qquad (C.14)$$

From (C.13) we know that (C.14) can be written as

$$E\{y_i(\mathbf{x} - \mathbf{w}_i)\} = 0 \qquad (C.15)$$

For simplicity, we use Y_{ij} to represent the stable output activity for neuron i when the input vector falls into the Voronoi region V_j for neuron j, or equivalently $Y_{ij} = \Phi(\|l_i - l_j\|)$, when j is the selected neuron. Let $P(j)$ denote the probability that $\mathbf{x}$ falls into V_j. Let $\mathcal{N}_i$ be the neighborhood for neuron i. Now we have

$$E\{y_i(\mathbf{x} - \widehat{\mathbf{w}}_i)\} = \sum_{j \in \mathcal{N}_i} P(j)Y_{ij}(E\{\mathbf{x}|\mathbf{x} \in V_j\} - \widehat{\mathbf{w}}_i) = 0.$$

Hence

$$\widehat{\mathbf{w}}_i \sum_{j \in \mathcal{N}_i} P(j)Y_{ij} = \sum_{j \in \mathcal{N}_i} P(j)Y_{ij}E\{\mathbf{x}|\mathbf{x} \in V_j\},$$

and therefore,

$$\begin{aligned}
\widehat{\mathbf{w}}_i &= \frac{\sum_{j \in \mathcal{N}_i} P(j)Y_{ij}E\{\mathbf{x}|\mathbf{x} \in V_j\}}{\sum_{j \in \mathcal{N}_i} P(j)Y_{ij}} \\
&= \frac{\int_{\Omega_i} p(\mathbf{x})y_i(\mathbf{x})\mathbf{x}d\mathbf{x}}{\int_{\Omega_i} p(\mathbf{x})y_i(\mathbf{x})d\mathbf{x}};
\end{aligned}$$

thus the proof. $\diamond$

Appendix D

Operational Measures

In this appendix, I summarize all the operational measures used in this dissertation.

D.1   Averaging Mechanism

Theorem D.1 :

$\{\xi[n]\}$ *is a random process. Let*

$$\bar{\xi}[n]_\gamma \triangleq \frac{\sum_{m=0}^{n} \gamma^m \xi[n-m]}{\sum_{m=0}^{n} \gamma^m} \qquad (D.1)$$

and

$$\widehat{\xi}[n]_\gamma \triangleq \gamma\widehat{\xi}[n-1]_\gamma + (1-\gamma)\xi[n], \qquad (D.2)$$

then $\widehat{\xi}[n]_\gamma \to \bar{\xi}[n]_\gamma$ in the following way:

$$Err[n] \triangleq \frac{\bar{\xi}[n]_\gamma - \widehat{\xi}[n]_\gamma}{\bar{\xi}[n]_\gamma} = \gamma^{n+1}. \qquad (D.3)$$

By repetitively applying (D.2) to substitute $\widehat{\xi}$ by the right hand side of (D.2), $\widehat{\xi}[n]_\gamma$ can be rewritten as

$$
\begin{aligned}
\widehat{\xi}[n]_\gamma &= (1-\gamma)\xi[n] + \gamma((1-\gamma)\xi[n-1] + \gamma\widehat{\xi}[n-2]_\gamma) \\
&= (1-\gamma)(\xi[n] + \gamma\xi[n-1] + \ldots + \gamma^n\xi[0]) \\
&= (1-\gamma)(\sum_{m=0}^{n} \gamma^m \xi[n-m]) \\
&= (1-\gamma^{n+1})\frac{\sum_{m=0}^{n}\gamma^m\xi[n-m]}{\sum_{m=0}^{n}\gamma^m} \\
&= (1-\gamma^{n+1})\overline{\xi}[n]_\gamma.
\end{aligned}
$$

Hence

$$
\frac{\overline{\xi}[n]_\gamma - \widehat{\xi}[n]_\gamma}{\overline{\xi}[n]_\gamma} = \gamma^{n+1} = Err[n],
$$

thus the proof.   ◇

Theorem D.1 states that the averaging mechanism $\widehat{\xi}[n]_\gamma$ used throughout this monograph very accurately measures of the weighted average $\overline{\xi}[n]_\gamma$ for the random process $\{\xi\}$. Theorem D.1 also suggests ways of determining γ to control the temporal window size. Suppose we want an equivalent window size of L; the rule of thumb is to set γ as

$$
\gamma = e^{\ln \epsilon / L} \tag{D.4}
$$

where ϵ is the cutoff threshold for the averaging process. Normally ϵ is chosen to be close to 0.

D.2 Summary of Operational Measures

mbol	Equation	Meaning	Where
$\widetilde{WD}_i[n]$	$\gamma_w \widehat{WD}_i[n-1] + (1-\gamma_w)\|\mathbf{w}_i[n] - \mathbf{w}_i[n-1]\|$	Walking Distance	Ch2
$\widetilde{VA}_i[n]$	$\gamma_v \widehat{VA}_i[n-1] + (1-\gamma_v)\|y_i[n] - \widehat{Act}_i[n]\|^2$	Activity Variance	Ch2
$\widetilde{Act}_i[n]$	$\gamma_a \widehat{Act}_i[n-1] + (1-\gamma_a)y_i[n]$	Output Activity	Ch2
$\widetilde{WD}_i^{l}[n]$	$|\delta_i^{(l)}|\,\|Q^{(l-1)}\|\,\widehat{WD}_i^{(l)}$	Fluctuated Distortion	Ch3, AppB
$\widetilde{d}_i[n_i^k]$	$\gamma_d \widehat{d}_i[n_i^{k-1}] + (1-\gamma_d)\|\mathbf{x}[n_i^k] - \mathbf{w}_i[n_i^{k-1}]\|$	Distortion	Ch4
$\widetilde{P}_i[n_i^k]$	$\gamma_p \widehat{P}_i[n_i^{k-1}] + (1-\gamma_p)/(n_i^k - n_i^{k-1})$	Probability	Ch4

Appendix E

Glossary of Symbols and Acronyms

$\triangleq$	By definition
$\exists$	There exists (existence quantifier)
$\forall$	For all (universal quantifier)
$\cap$	Set intersection
$\cup$	Set conjunction
$\in$	Belong to
$\subseteq$	Subset relation (of sets)
$\supseteq$	Superset relation (of sets)
$\neg$	Logical NOT
$\vee$	Logical OR
$\wedge$	Logical AND
$\approx$	Approximately equal
$\eta[t]$	The instance of the object η at time t. η can be a variable, function, structure, etc.

$\eta[*]$	The instance of the object η at the current time index
$<\eta>, \bar{\eta}$	The expectation value of the variable η
$\sigma^{(n)}(x)$	The nth derivative of the function $\sigma(x)$
Act_i	The output activity measure for the neuron i
$Arg(f)$	The number of input arguments of the function f
BDN	Bi-Directional Neuron
BS	Base Set
CS	Composite State
$Dim(\vec{x})$	Dimensionality of the vector $\vec{x}$
DSN	Distributed S-level Network
$Dup(Z^n, \mathcal{G})$	$\underbrace{(v_n, v_n, \ldots, v_n)}\|\mathcal{G}\|v_n s, v_n \in Z^n$ (duplicating the same vector $v_n \ \|\mathcal{G}\|$ times, $v_n \in Z^n$
$E\{X\}$	Expectation value of the random variable X
E-Space	Neural Network Structure Evolution Space
$\mathcal{F}^n$	An n-dimensional space over the field $\mathcal{F}$. $\mathcal{F}$ can be $\mathcal{Z}$ (the set of integers), $\mathcal{R}$ (the set of real numbers), etc.
FBP	Feed Back Path
FD_i	The Fluctuated Distortion Measure for neuron i
FFP	Feed Forward Path
FLA	Function Level Adaptation
FN	Formal Neuron
F-Net	Function level neural network

FS	Function Space
FUNNET	FUNction NETwork
IAS	Input Argument Set
ICM	Input Connection Map
$In(N)[t]$	The values of the input vector for the object N at time t. N can be a neuron, a network element, or a neural network.
I-Set	Input Set
LNN	Lattice Neural Network
MBS	Minimum Base Set
MF	Modulating Function
MPS	Modulating Parameter Structure
NE	Network Element
NF	Node Function
NIE	Network Input Element
NOE	Network Output Element
NPS	Neuron Parameter Space
NSEE	Network Structure Evolution Element
OCM	Output Connection Map
$Out(N)[t]$	The output value of the object N at time t. N can be a neuron, a network object, or a neural network.
O-Set	Output Set
PAA	Parameter Adaptation Automata
PAF	Parameter Adjustment Function

PCS	Parameter Control State
PF	Projective Field
PFT	Parameterized Function Tree
PK	Processing Kernel
PLA	Parameter Level Adaptaion
P-Net	Parameter level neural network
POP	Primitive Operator
POS	Primitive Operator Set
PSTF	Parameter State Transition Function
PTV	Primitive Translation Vector
R	The Set of real numbers
RSCV	Received Evolution Control Vector
RFBS	Received Feed Back Signal
RF	Receptive Field
SCS	Structure Control State
SEA	Structure Evolution Automata
SEAL	Structure Evolution Action List
SLA	Structure Level Adaptation
S-Net	Structure level neural network
SOFM	Self-Organization Feature Map
SOP	Structure Operator
SOS	Spanning Operator Set
SOSF	Structure Operator Selection Function

SPAN	Space PArtition Network
SSTF	Structure State Transition Function
STF	State Transition Function
TFBS	Transmitting Feed Back Signal
TFBV	Transmitting Feed Back Vector
TSCV	Transmitting Structure Control Vector
UDN	Uni-Directional Neuron
VA_i	Activity Variance for the neuron i
VQ	Vector Quantization
$\underline{W}$	A matrix
$\underline{W}^{l-1,l}$	The weight matrix between layers $l-1$ and l in a multi-layer feed-forward networks
$w_{ij}^{l-1,l}$	The interconnection weight between the neurons j in layer $l-1$ and the neuron i in layer l
WD_i	Walking Distance for the neuron i
Y^T	The transpose of a matrix or a vector Y
$\mathcal{Z}$	The set of integers
$\mathcal{Z}^+$	The set of positive integers

Bibliography

[1] *Proc. IEEE First International Conference on Neural Networks,* IEEE (1987).

[2] *Proc. IEEE Second International Conference on Neural Networks,* IEEE (1988).

[3] *Proc. International Joint Conference on Neural Networks,* IEEE & INNS (1989).

[4] *Proc. IEEE First Conference on Neural Information Processing Systems Natural and Synthetic,* in Anderson, Dana Z. (Ed.) *Neural Information Processing Systems,* American Institute of Physics, New York (1988).

[5] *Abstracts of the International Neural Network Society First Annual Meeting,* INNS (1988).

[6] Special Issue on Neural Networks, *Applied Optics, Vol.26, No.23* (December 1987).

[7] Special Section on Neural Networks, *IEEE Tran. on Acoustics, Speech, and Signal Processing, Vol.36, No.7,* pp.1107-1190 (July 1988).

[8] *Evolution, Games and Learning: Models for Adaptation in Machines and Nature, Proceedings of the Fifth Annual International Conference of the Center for Nonlinear Studies,* Los Almos, NM, USA, May 20-24, 1985, in *Physica D, Vol.22D, Nos.1-3* (1986).

[9] Ackley, David H.; Hinton, Geoffrey E.; and Sejnowski, Terrence J., "A Learning Algorithm for Boltzmann Machines," *Cognitive Science,* Vol.9, pp.147-169 (1985).

[10] Ahalt, Stanley C.; Chen, Prakoon; and Krishnamurthy, Ashok K., "Performance Analysis of Two Image Vector Quantization Techniques," *IJCNN: International Joint Conference on Neural Networks, conference proceedings* pp.I-16, (June 1989).

[11] Amari, S.-I., "Neural Theory of Association and Concept-Formation," *Biological Cybernetics, Vol.26,* pp.175-185 (1977).

[12] Amari, S.-I, "Topographic Organization of Nerve Fields," *Bull. Math. Biol., Vol.42,* pp.339-364 (1980).

[13] Anderson, James A. and Rosenfeld, Edward, *Neurocomputing: Foundation of Research,* MIT press, Cambridge, Mass. (1988).

[14] Anderson, J.A., "Neural Models with Cognitive Implications," In D. LaBerge & S. J. Samuels (Eds.) *Basic Processes in Reading Perception and Comprehension,* pp.27-90, Hillsdale, NJ., Erlbaum (1977).

[15] Anderson, J. A. and Mozer, M. C., "Categorization and Selective Neurons," in G. E. Hinton & J. A. Anderson (Eds.), Parallel Models of Associative Memory, pp.213-236, Hillsdale, NJ., Erlbaum (1981).

[16] Baron, Robert J., *The Cerebral Computer: an Introduction to the Computational Structure of Human Brain*, Hillsdale, NJ., L.Erlbaum Associates (1987).

[17] Berger, T., *Rate Distortion Theory*, Prentice-Hall Inc., Englewood Cliffs, NJ (1971).

[18] Block, H.D., "The Perceptron: a Model for Brain Functioning I ," *Review of Modern Physics, Vol.34*, pp.123-135 (1962).

[19] Carpenter, Gail and Grossberg, Stehen, "A Massively Parallel Architecture for a Self-Organizing Neural Pattern Recognition Machine," *Computer Vision, Graphics, and Image Processing. Vol.37*, pp.54-114 (1987), also Stephen Grossberg (Ed.) *Neural Networks and Natural Intelligence*, Chap.6, Cambridge, Mass., MIT Press (1988).

[20] Chang, Pao-Chi *Predictive, Hierarchical, and Transform vector Quantization for Speech Coding*, Ph.D dissertation, Stanford University, Stanford, CA. (May 1986).

[21] Chou, Philip A.; Lookabaugh, Tom; and Gray, Robert, "Optimal Pruning with Applications to Tree-Structured Source Coding and Modeling," *IEEE Tran. Information Theory*, Vol.35, No.2, pp.299-315 (March 1989).

[22] Chou, Philip A., *Application of Information Theory to Pattern Recognition and the design of Decision Trees and Trellises*, Ph.D. dissertation, Stanford University, Stanford, CA. (June 1988).

[23] Chou, Philip A., "The Capacity of the Kanerva Associative Memory," *IEEE Proc. on Information Theory, Vol.35, No.2*, pp.281-298 (March 1989).

[24] Cohen, Michael; Grossberg, Stephen, "Masking fields: a Massively Parallel Neural Architecture for Learning, Recognizing, and Predicting Multiple Groupings of Patterned Data," *Applied Optics, Vol.26, No.10*, pp.54-115 (May 1987), also in Stephen Grossberg (Ed.) *Neural Networks and Natural Intelligence*, Chap.7, , MIT Press, Cambridge, Mass. (1988).

[25] Conway, J.H.; and Sloane, N.J.A. Sloane,"Voronoi Regions of Lattices, Second Moments of Polytopes, and Quantization," *IEEE Tran. Information Theory*, Vol.IT-28, No.2, pp.211-226 (March 1982).

[26] Conway, J.H.; and Sloane, N.J.A., "Fast Quantizing and Decoding Algorithms for Lattice Quantizers and Codes," *IEEE Tran. Information Theory*, Vol.IT-28, No.2, pp.227-232 (March 1982).

[27] Cornsweet, T.N., *Visual Perception*, New York, Academic Press, pp.270-310 (1970).

[28] Cybento, G., "Approximation by Superpositions of a Sigmoidal Function," *Mathematics of Control, Signals, and Systems*, Springer-Verlag New York Inc. (1989).

[29] *DARPA Neural Network Study*, AFCEA International Press, Fairfax, Virginia (Nov. 1988).

[30] Dunham, Mari Ostendorf, *Finite-State Vector Quantization for Low Rate Speech Coding*, Ph.D. dissertation, Stanford University, Stanford, CA. (Feb. 1985).

[31] Edelman, Gerald M., *Neural Darwinism: The Theory of Neuronal Group Selection*, Basic Books, NY (1987).

[32] Edelman, Gerald M., *Topobiology: An Introduction to Molecular Embryology*, Basic Books, NY (1988).

[33] Eigen, M. and Schuster, P., *The Hypercycle: A Principle of Natural Self-Organization*, Springer-Verlag, NY (1979).

[34] El-Leithy, Nevine and Newcomb, Robert W., Guest Editors, "Special Issue on Neural Networks," *IEEE Tran. Circuits and Systems, Vol.36, No.5*, (May 1989).

[35] Feldman, J. A. and Ballard, D.H., "Connectionist Models and Their Properties," *Cognitive Science*, Vol.6, pp.205-254 (1982).

[36] Feldman, J. A., "Energy Methods in Connectionist Modeling," in P. A. Devijver and J. Kittler (Eds.), *Pattern Recognition Theory and Applications*, NATO ASI Series, Vol.F30, Springer-Verlag, Berlin Heidelberg (1987).

[37] Foster, John, *Finite-State-Vector Quantization for Waveform Coding*, Ph.D. dissertation, Stanford University, Stanford, CA. (Nov. 1982).

[38] Fukushima, Kunihiko; Miyake, Sei; and Ito, Takayuki, "Neocognitron: a Neural Network Model for a Mechanism of Visual Pattern Recognition," *IEEE Tran. on Systems, Man, and Cybernetics, Vol.13*, pp.826-834 (1983).

[39] Gallager, R.G., *Information Theory and Reliable Communication*, John Wiley & Sons, NY (1968).

[40] Geman, Stuart and Geman, Donald, "Stochastic Relaxation, Gibbs Distributions, and the Bayesian Restoration of Images," *IEEE*

Tran. Pattern Analysis and Machine Intelligence, Vol.PAMI-6, pp.721-741 (1984).

[41] Gersho, Allen and Cuperman, Vladimir, "Vector Quantization: A Pattern-Matching Technique for Speech Coding," *IEEE Communication Magazine,* December, pp.15-21 (1983).

[42] Gersho, Allen, "On the Structure of Vector Quantizers," *IEEE Tran. Information Theory,* Vol.IT-28, No.2, pp.157-166 (March 1982).

[43] Gersho, Allen, "Asymptotically Optimal Block Quantization," *IEEE Tran. Information Theory,* Vol.IT-25, No.4, pp.373-380 (July 1979).

[44] Gersho, Allen Gersho and Gray, Robert M., *Vector Quantization and Signal Compression,* Kluwer Academic Publishers, (1990).

[45] Graubard, Stephen R., Editor, *The Artificial Intelligence Debate: False Starts, Real Foundations,* The MIT Press, Cambridge, Mass. (1988).

[46] Gray, Robert M., "Vector Quantization," *IEEE ASSP Magazine,* April, pp.4-29 (1984).

[47] Robert M. Gray, *Source Coding Theory,* Kluwer Academic Publishers, (1990).

[48] Robert M. Gray and Lee D. Davisson, *Random Processes,* Prentice-Hall, Inc. (1986).

[49] Grossberg, S, "Adaptive Pattern Classification and Universal Recoding: Part I. Parallel Development and Coding of Neural Feature Detectors," *Biological Cybernetics,* Vol.23, pp.121-134 (1976).

[50] Hebb, Donald O., *The Organization of Behavior*, New York, Wiley (1949).

[51] Hodgkin, A. L. and Huxley, A. F., "Measurement of Current-Voltage Relationships in the Membrane of the Giant Axon of Loligo," *Journal of Physiology, Vol.116,* pp.424 (1952).

[52] Hodgkin, A. L. and Huxley, A. F., "Current Carried by Sodium and Potassiun Ions Through the Membrane of the Giant Axon of Loligo," *Journal of Physiology, Vol.116,* pp.449 (1952).

[53] Hopfield, J. J. "Neural Networks and Physical Systems with Emergent Collective Computational Abilities," *Proceedings of the National Academy of Sciences,* Vol.79, pp.2554-2558, (1982).

[54] Hopfield, J. J. "Neurons with Graded Response have Collective Computation Properties Like Those of Two-State Neurons," *Proceedings of the National Academy of Sciences,* Vol.81, pp.3088-3092.

[55] Hopkins, W. G. and Brown, M. C., *Development of Nerve Cells and Their Connections,* Cambridge University Press, (1984).

[56] Hoyenga, Katharine Blick and Hoyenga, Kermit T., *Psychobiology: The Neuron and Behavior,* Brooks/Core Publishing Co. (1988).

[57] Hubel, D.H. and Wiesel, T.N., "Receptive Fields, Binocular Interaction and Functional Architecture in the Cat's Visual Cortex," *Journal of Physiology, Vol.160,* pp.106-154 (1962).

[58] Hubel, D.H. and Wiesel, T,N., "Receptive Fields and Functional Architecture of Monkey Striate Cortex," *Journal of Physiology, Vol.195,* pp.215-243 (1968).

[59] Hubel, D.H. and Wiesel, T.N., "Sequence Regularity and Geometry of Orientation Columns in the Monkey Striate Cortex," *Journal of Comparative Neurology, Vol.158,* pp.267-294 (1974).

[60] James, William, *Psychology (Briefer Course),* New York, Holt, Chapter XVI, "Association," pp.253-279 (1890).

[61] Kirkpatrick, S.; Gelatt, C.D., Jr.; and Vecchi, M.P., "Optimization by Simulated Annealing," *Science,* Vol.220, pp.671-681 (1984).

[62] Kittel, Charles, *Introduction to Solid State Physics,* 6th ed., Chap.1, Wiley (1986).

[63] Kittel, Charles and Kroemer, Herbert, *Thermal Physics,* 2nd ed., W. H. Freeman and Company, San Francisco, CA. (1980).

[64] Kohonen, Teuvo, "Correlation Matrix Memories," *IEEE Tran. on Computers, Vol.21,* pp.353-359 (1972).

[65] Kohonen, Teuvo, "Self-Organized Formation of Topologically Correct Feature Maps," *Biological Cybernetics,* Vol.43, pp.59-69 (1982).

[66] Kohonen, Teuvo, *"Self Organization and Associative Memory,"* *Chap 5*, pp.119-155.

[67] Kohonen, Teuvo, "The Neural Phonetic Typewriter," *Computer,* pp.11-22, (March 1988).

[68] Kohonen, Teuvo, "An Introduction to Neural Computing," *Neural Networks,* Vol.1, No.1, pp.3-16 (1988)

[69] Kolmogorov, A. N., "On the Representation of Continuous Functions of Many Variables by Superposition of Continuous Functions

of One Variables and Addition," *Dokl. Akad. Nauk. SSSR,* Vol.114, pp.953-956 (1957).

[70] Kuffler, Stephen W.; Nicholls, John G.; and Martin, A. Robert, *From Neuron to Brain: A Cellular Approach to the Function of the Nervous System,* 2nd Ed., Sunderland, Mass., Sinauer Associates (1984).

[71] Kung, H.T., "Panel on Future Directions in Parallel Computer Architecture, the 16th Annual International Symposium on Computer Architecture," collected in *ACM SIGARCH, Computer Architecture News, Vol.17, No.4* (June 1989).

[72] Kunt, M.; Ikonomopoulos, A.; and Kocher, M., "Second-Generation Image-Coding Techniques," *Proceedings of the IEEE, Vol.73, No.4,* pp.496-848 (April 1985).

[73] Langton, Christopher G., Editor, *Artificial Life,* Addison-Wesley Publishing Company (1988).

[74] Lashley, K.S., "In Search of the Engram," *Society of Experimental Biology Symposium, No.4: Psychological Mechanisms in Animal Behavior,* Cambridge, England, Cambridge University Press, pp.454-455, 468-473, 477-480 (1950).

[75] Lee, Tsu-chang and Peterson, Allen M., "Adaptive Vector Quantization Using a Self-Development Neural Network," IEEE Journal on Selected Areas in Communications, Vol.8, No.8, pp.1458-1471 (October, 1990).

[76] Lee, Tsu-chang and Peterson, Allen M., "Adaptive Signal Processing with a Self-Development Neural Network," in *Proceedings of*

1989 International Symposium on VLSI Technology, Systems, and Applications (May, 1989).

[77] Lee, Tsu-chang and Peterson, Allen M., "SPAN: A Neural Network That Grows," 1st International Joint Conference on Neural Networks (June, 1989).

[78] Lee, Tsu-chang and Peterson, Allen M., "Implementing a Self-Development Neural Network Using Doubly Linked Lists," in *Proceedings of COMPSAC89,* IEEE 13th International Computer Software & Application Conference (September, 1989).

[79] Lee, Tsu-chang; Peterson, Allen M.; and Jhy-Cherng Tsai, "A Multi-Layer Feed-Forward Neural Network With Dynamically Adjustable Structure," in *Conference Proceedings, 1990 IEEE International Conference on Systems, Man, and Cybernetics,* pp.367 (November, 1990).

[80] Linde Y.; Buzo, A.; and Gray, R. M., "An Algorithm for Vector Quantizer Design," *IEEE Tran. Commun.,* Vol.COM-28, No.1, pp.84-95 (Jan. 1980).

[81] Lloyd, Stuart P, "Least Square Quantization in PCM," *Bell Laboratories Technical Notes,* (1957), Published in *IEEE Tran. Information Theory,* Vol.IT28, No.2, pp.129-137 (March 1982).

[82] Lookabaugh, Thomas Duncan, *Variable Rate and Adaptive Frequency Domain Vector Quantization of Speech,* Ph.D. Dissertation, Stanford University, Stanford, CA. (June 1988).

[83] Lorentz, G. G., "The 13th problem of Hilbert," *Proceedings of Symposia in Pure Mathematics,* Vol.28, pp.419-430 (1976).

[84] MacGregor, Ronald J., *Neural and Brain Modeling*, Academic Press, 1987.

[85] Malsburg, Ch. von der, "Self-Organization of Orientation Sensitive Cells in the Striate Cortex," *Kybernetik, Vol.14*, pp.85-100 (1973).

[86] Malsburg, Ch. von der and Willshaw, D.J., "How to Label Nerve Cells so that They can Interconnect in an Ordered Fashion," *Proc. Natl. Acad. Sci. USA, Vol.74*, pp.5176-5178 (1977).

[87] Marr, D. and Poggio, T., "Cooperative Computation of Stereo Disparity," *Science, Vol.194*, pp.283-287.

[88] Marr, David, *Vision*, San Francisco: W.H. Freeman, pp,19-38,pp.54-61, (1982).

[89] McCulloch, Warren S. and Pitts, Walter, "A Logical Calculus of the Ideas Immanent in Nervous Activity," *Bulletin of Mathematical Biophysics, Vol.5*, pp.115-133 (1943).

[90] McEliece, Robert, et al., "The Capacity of the Hopfield Associative Memory," *IEEE Tran. on Information Theory*, Vol.IT-33, No.4, pp.461-482, (July 1987).

[91] Mead, Carver and Conway, Lynn, *Introduction to VLSI systems*, Addison-Wesley, Reading, Mass. (1980).

[92] Mead, Carver, *Analog VLSI and Neural Systems*, Addison-Wesley (1989).

[93] Messerschmitt, David G., "Communications in VLSI," in *6th International Workshop: Microelectronics and Photonics in Communications*, Abstracts & Papers (June 1989).

[94] Mezard, Marc; Parisi, Giorgio; and Virasoro, Miguel Angel (Eds), *Spin Glass Theory and Beyond,* World Scientific Lecture Notes in Physics, Vol.9., NJ, World Scientific (1987).

[95] Minsky, Marvin and Papert, Seymour, *Perceptrons,* Cambridge, MA: MIT Press, 1969.

[96] Mountcastle, V.B., "Modality and Topographic Properties of Single Neurons of Cat's Somatic Sensory Cortex," *Journal of Neurophysiology, Vol.20,* pp.408-434 (1957).

[97] Nasrabadi, Nasser M., "Image Coding Using Vector Quantization: A Review," *IEEE Tran. Comm.,* Vol.36, No.8, pp.957-971 (Aug. 1988).

[98] Nasrabadi, Nasser M. and Feng, Yushu, "Vector Quantization of Images Based upon a Neural-Network Clustering Algorithm," *SPIE Vol.1001: Visual Communications and Image Processing'88, Part 1,* pp.207-213 (Nov. 1988).

[99] Nasrabadi, Nasser M. and Feng, Yushu, "Vector Quantization of Images Based upon the Kohonen Self-Organization Feature Maps," *IEEE International Conference on Neural Networks, conference proceedings,* pp.I-93 (July 1988).

[100] Neumann, John von, *Theory of Self-Reproducing Automata: edited and completed by Arthur W. Burks,* University of Illinois Press, Urbana and London (1966).

[101] Nilson, N.J., *Learning Machines - Foundations of Trainable Pattern Classifying Systems,* New York, McGraw-Hill (1965).

[102] Packard, N. and Wolfram, S., "Two-Dimensional Cellular Automata," *J. Stat. Phys., Vol.38,* pp.901 (1985).

[103] Pitts, Walter and McCulloch, Warren S., "How We Know Universals: the Perception of Auditory and Visual Forms," *Bulletin of Mathematical Biophysics, Vol.9,* pp.127-147 (1947).

[104] Reichl, L. E., *A Modern Course in Statistical Physics,* University of Texas Press (1980).

[105] Ritter, H. and Schulten, K., "Convergence Properties of Kohonen's Topology Conserving Maps: Fluctuations, Stability and Dimension Selection," *Biological Cybernetics, Vol.60,* pp.59-71 (1988).

[106] Rumelhart, David E. and McClelland, James L., *Parallel Distributed Processing: Explorations in the Microstructure of Cognition, Vol.1: Foundations,* MIT Press, Cambridge, Mass. (1986).

[107] Rumelhart, David E. and McClelland, James L., *Parallel Distributed Processing: Explorations in the Microstructure of Cognition, Vol.2: Psychological and Biological Models,* MIT Press, Cambridge, Mass. (1986).

[108] Rumelhart, D. E.; Hinton, G. E.; and Williams, R. J., "Learning Internal Representations by Error Propagation," *Parallel Distributed Processing: Explorations in the Microstructures of Cognition,* Vol.I, D.E. Rumelhart and J.L. McClelland (Eds.), Cambridge, MA: MIT Press, pp.318-362.

[109] Rumelhart, D. E.; Hinton, Geoffrey E.; and Williams, Ronald J., "Learning Representations by Back-Propagating errors," *Nature* 323: pp.533-536.

[110] Posner, M.I., *Chronometric Exploration of Mind*, Hillsdale, NJ., Lawrence Erlbaum Associates (1978).

[111] Reale, R.A. and Imig, T.J., "Tonotopic Organization in Auditory Cortex of the Cat," *J. of Comp. Neurol., Vol.192*, pp.265-291 (1980).

[112] Rissanen, J., "Minimum Description Length Principle," in S. Kotz and N.L. Johnson (Eds.), *Encyclopedia of Statistical Sciences V*, pp.523-527, Wiley, New York (1985).

[113] Rissanen, J., "Stochastic Complexity and the MDL Principle," *Econometric Review, No.1*, pp.85-102 (1987).

[114] Rissanen, J., "Understanding the 'Go' of It," IBM Research Magazine, (Winter 1988).

[115] Rissanen, J., "Stochastic Complexity and Sufficient Statistics," Tech. Rep. K54/802, IBM Research Laboratory, San Jose, CA. (1986).

[116] Rosenblatt, F., "The Perceptron: a Probabilistic Model for Information Storage and Organization in the Brain," *Psychological Review, Vol.65*, pp.386-408 (1958).

[117] Saund, Eric, "Dimensionality-Reduction Using Connectionist Networks," *IEEE Tran. Pattern Analysis and Machine Intelligence, Vol.11, No.3*, (March 1989).

[118] Schartz, Jocob T., "The New Connectionism: Developing Relationships Between Neuroscience and Artificial Intelligence," in Stephen Graubard (Ed.) *The Artificial Intelligence Debate: False Starts, Real Foundations*, Cambridge, Mass., MIT Press (1988).

[119] Schwartz, M.F.; Martin, O.S.M.; and Saffran, E.M., "Dissociations of Language Function in Dementia: a Case Study," *Brain and Language, Vol. 7,* pp.277-306 (1979).

[120] Seelen, W. von; Shaw, G.; and U.M. Leinhos, Editors, *Organization of Neural Networks: Structures and Models,* VCH Verlagsgesellschaft mbH, D-6940 Weinheim, FRG (1988).

[121] Selfridge, O. G., "Pandemonium: a Paradigm for Learning," *Mechanisation of Thought Processes: Proceedings of a Symposium Held at the National Physical Laboratory,* pp.513-526, London, HMSO (Nov.1958).

[122] Shannon, C.E., "A Mathematical Theory of Communication," *Bell Systems Technical Journal,* Vol.27, pp.379-423, 623-656 (1948).

[123] Shannon, C.E., "Coding Theorem for a Discrete Source with a Fidelity Criterion," *IRE National Convention Record, Part 4,* pp.142-163 (1959).

[124] Shepherd, G.M., *The Synaptic Organization of the Brain,* 2nd ed., New York, Oxford University Press (1979).

[125] Shepherd, G.M., "Microcircuits in the Nervous System," *Scientific American, Vol.238, No.2,* pp.93 (Feb. 1978).

[126] Shoham, Yair and Gersho, Allen; "Efficient Bit Allocation for An Arbitrary Set of Quantizers," *IEEE Tran. Acoustic Speech and Signal Processing,* Vol.36, No.9, pp. 1445-1453 (Sept. 1988).

[127] Shriver, Bruce D., Guest Editor, "Artificial Neural Systems," *Computer, Vol.21, No.3,* (March 1988).

[128] Tolat, Viral V. and Peterson, Allen M., "A Self-Organizing Neural Network for Classifying Sequences," *Proceedings of IJCNN*, pp.II-561 (June 1989).

[129] Tolat, Viral V., *A Self-Organizing Neural Network for Representing Sequences*, Ph.D. Dissertation, Stanford University, Stanford, CA. (Aug. 1989).

[130] Towe, A., "Notes on the Hypothesis of Columnar Organization in Somatosensory Cerebral Cortex," *Brain Behav. Evol., Vol.11*, pp.16-47 (1975).

[131] Aho, Alfred V.; Hopcroft, John E.; and Ullman, D. Jeffrey, *The Design and Analysis of Computer Algorithms*, Addison-Wesley Pub. Co., Mass. (1974).

[132] Viterbi, A.J. and Omura, J.K., *Principles of Digital Communication and Coding*, McGraw-Hill Book Company, New York (1979).

[133] Werbos, P. J., "Maximizing Long-Term Gas Industry Profits in Two Minutes in Lotus Using Neural Network Methods," *IEEE Tran. on System, Man, and Cybernetics, Vol.19, No.2*, pp.315-333 (March 1989).

[134] Widrow, Bernard and Hoff, Marcian E., "Adaptive Switching Circuits," *1960 IRE WESCON Convention Record*, New York, pp.96-104 (1960).

[135] Widrow, Bernard; Gupta, N. K.; and Maitra, S., "Punish/Reward: Learning With a Critic in Adaptive Threshold Systems," *IEEE Tran. on Systems, Man, and Cybernetics, Vol.3*, pp.455-465 (1973).

[136] Willshaw, D.J. and Malsburg, Ch. von der, "How Patterned Neural Connections Can be Set Up by Self-Organization," *Proc. R. Soc.*, *B194*, pp.431-445 (1976).

[137] Willshaw, D.J. and Malsburg, Ch. von der, "A Marker Induction Mechanism for the Establishment of Ordered Neural Mapping; Its Application to the Retino-Tectal Problem," *Phil. Trans. R. Soc. Lond.*, *B287*, pp.203-243 (1979).

[138] Winter, Rodney, *MADLINE Rule II: A New Method for Training Networks of ADALINEs*, Ph.D. Dissertation, Stanford University, Stanford, CA. (1989).

[139] Wolfram, S., "Statistical Mechanics of Cellular Automata," *Rev. Mod. Phys.*, *Vol.55*, pp.601 (1983).

[140] Wood, John W. and O'Neil, Sean D., "Subband Coding of Images," *IEEE Tran. Acoustic, Speech, and Signal Processing, Vol.ASSP-34, No.5*, pp.1278-1288 (Oct. 1986).

[141] Yates, F. Eugene (Ed.), *Self-Organizing Systems: The Emergence of Order*, Plenum Press, NY. (1987).

Index